WHERE NEXT?

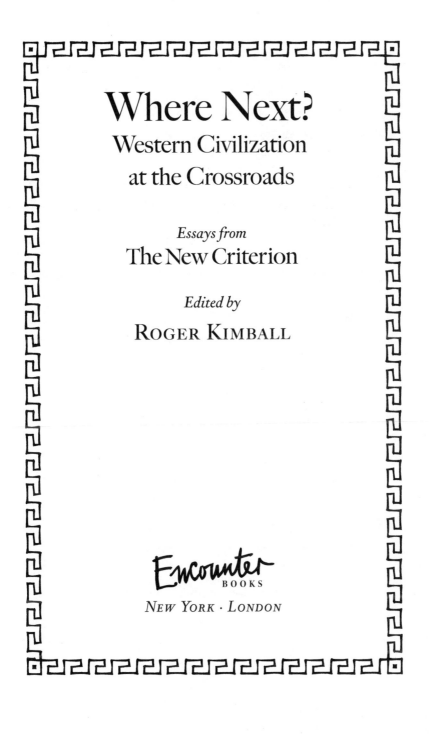

Where Next?
Western Civilization at the Crossroads

Essays from
The New Criterion

Edited by

ROGER KIMBALL

Encounter
BOOKS

NEW YORK · LONDON

First American edition published in 2022 by Encounter Books, an activity of
Encounter for Culture and Education, Inc., a nonprofit, tax-exempt corporation.
Encounter Books website address: www.encounterbooks.com

Manufactured in the United States and printed on acid-free paper.
The paper used in this publication meets the minimum requirements of
ANSI/NISO Z39.48 – 1992 (R 1997) (Permanence of Paper).

FIRST AMERICAN EDITION

LIBRARY OF CONGRESS CATALOGING-IN-PUBLICATION DATA

Names: Kimball, Roger, 1953– editor.
Title: Where next?: Western civilization at the crossroads /
edited by Roger Kimball.
Description: First American edition. | New York, New York: Encounter Books,
2022. | Includes bibliographical references and index.
Identifiers: LCCN 2022023655 (print) | LCCN 2022023656 (ebook) |
ISBN 9781641773157 (cloth) | ISBN 9781641773164 (ebook)
Subjects: LCSH: Civilization, Western.
Classification: LCC CB245 .W514 2022 (print) | LCC CB245 (ebook) |
DDC 909/.09821—dc23/eng/20220727
LC record available at https://lccn.loc.gov/2022023655
LC ebook record available at https://lccn.loc.gov/2022023656

1 2 3 4 5 6 7 8 9   20 22

In memoriam
JAMES F. PENROSE 1952–2022

Quid sit futurum cras fuge quærere
et quem Fors dierum cumque
dabit lucro appone

CONTENTS

Introduction

ROGER KIMBALL

THE TEN ESSAYS IN *Where Next?* began life as a series of reflections in *The New Criterion* to mark its fortieth anniversary season in 2021–22. They have been edited and revised for inclusion in this volume. A little like Akira Kurosawa's film *Rashomon*, they offer different perspectives on a single complex phenomenon, summarized in our subtitle "Western Civilization at the Crossroads."

It would be paltering with the truth to say that this book offers a definitive answer to the question posed in its title. Such questions, I hasten to add, almost never admit of pat answers. Nevertheless, its wide-ranging and multifaceted inquiries into the state of the West *circa* 2022 do offer a vivid if unsystematic spiritual anatomy of our times. One important leitmotif in this book is sounded by the historians Allen C. Guelzo and James Hankins in "Civilization & Tradition," the essay that inaugurated our series in *The New Criterion* and the chapter that introduces this volume. It is a theme that is as simple to state as it is impossible to unfold fully. It has something to do with memory, which involves not just a simple registering of what had gone before us but also an active engagement with its pressures and challenges. There is a reason that Plato yoked recollection (ἀνάμνησις) and learning, and there is a reason that cultural amnesia has from time immemorial been associated with civilizational decay.

The theme of Guelzo and Hankins's argument also has something to do with the union named in their title, "Civilization & Tradition." That conjunction signals not so much a finished state as a process of mutual implication fueled by the delivery implicit in the action of "tradition," i.e., that which is handed down, *traditum*, from the past.

That might seem to be a simple or an obvious point. *Of course* civilization depends upon a thoughtful – which means, in part, a not uncritical – nurturing of the traditions out of which it arose. But when one considers what a deep and concerted attack there is in Western societies on the multifarious deposit of the *traditum*, then one is reminded that it is often the simplest questions that take us most deeply into a subject. Guelzo and Hankins adduce various prerequisites for the perpetuation of civilization, "Above all," they stress, preservation of the

> moral and spiritual resources that generate loyalty to recognized authorities and allow individuals to actualize their full potential as human beings. The spiritual resources of a civilization provide those who share them with an identity that transcends the identity belonging to individual peoples united merely by common descent (the premodern meaning of "nation," *natio* in Latin). They produce a common culture that may last many centuries and even outlive the collapse of civilizational order.

It is sobering to recognize the extent to which we have been making withdrawals on the spiritual account of our civilization without assuring that corresponding or reparative deposits were being

INTRODUCTION

made to offset the losses and shore up that common, or once-common, culture.

"In recent times," Guelzo and Hankins observe, "we have seen spread through our schools and institutions an improper and uncivilized humility, a malicious form of humility indistinguishable from self-hatred. This is a humility that humiliates, that seeks to blind Westerners to their magnificent traditions and to rub their noses, like misbehaving dogs, in their worst offenses." Spinoza, following Euclid, would end his propositions with the label QED, *quod erat demonstrandum*: here is the thing that was to have been demonstrated. The institutions superintending our education might as well substitute the letters "BLM" or "CRT," indicating that their work of mockery or destruction has been accomplished.

Guelzo and Hankins also touch on another important feature of civilization that is blithely ignored by its spoiled and rancorous beneficiaries. "These attacks on Western civilization," they note, "illustrate a sad truth about all civilizations at all times: their fragility." Indeed. What took decades or even centuries to build up can be destroyed virtually overnight. Then – too late! – is it discovered that it is much easier to tear down than to build up.

This is a point that the political philosopher James Burnham underscored with his observation that "Suicide is probably more frequent than murder as the end phase of a civilization." What Burnham warned about, and what we are still conjuring with, is the seductive toxin that involves an awful failure of understanding which is also a mortal failure of nerve — a failure, that is to say, to grasp and inhabit those "spiritual resources" that Guelzo and Hankins identify as providing a "common culture" and shared identity.

INTRODUCTION

In his deep though curiously titled book *Physics and Politics* – it has nothing to do with physics, and politics enters only obliquely – Walter Bagehot traces the course of civilizations from savagery to "the age of discussion." We are not permitted to describe savage societies as "savage" any longer, which is one reason that Bagehot's book is no longer read with the intensity it deserves. But the censorious dictates of political correctness cannot obscure Bagehot's calm and commanding observation that "government by discussion" — "slow government" — is both "a principal organ for improving mankind" and "a plant of singular delicacy." The question of how best to nurture this delicate plant is Bagehot's central concern. It is also the concern of *Where Next?* Part of the answer lies in facing up to the unpalatable realities about power that make civilization possible. The other part lies in embracing what Bagehot calls "animated moderation," that "union of life with measure, of spirit with reasonableness," which assures that discussion will continue without descending into violence or anarchy. It seems like a small thing. But then achieved order always does – until it is lost.

I should like to take this opportunity to thank my colleagues at *The New Criterion* for their many labors. Jayne Allison, Caetlynn Booth, Jane Coombs, Robert Erickson, Adam Kirsch, James Panero, and Isaac Sligh have given local habitation and a name to our literary and critical ambitions, making the idea of *The New Criterion* a reality. Our visiting critics Conrad Black and Victor Davis Hanson not only contributed to this volume but also aided in the magazine's missionary work throughout our fortieth anniversary season. Benjamin Riley, our managing editor, deserves special thanks for overseeing the many editorial tasks involved in bringing this book to press. And Carl W. Scarbrough, book designer nonpareil, clothed our efforts in a suitably splendid typographical form. Finally, it is with sadness that I note the death in May 2022 of James F. Penrose, a frequent contributor to *The New Criterion* and a close friend of the editors. James made it to the biblically sanctioned age of seventy, but just barely. That used to seem like a venerable age. Now it seems like high middle age, the prime of life. We dedicate *Where Next?* to his memory. *Requiescat in pace.*

July 2022

Civilization & Tradition

Allen C. Guelzo & James Hankins

*We can never cut ourselves off from antiquity unless we
intend to revert to barbarism. The barbarian and
the creature of exclusively modern civilization
both live without history.*

Jacob Burckhardt

A CIVILIZATION IS a complex system of customs, practices,
and beliefs that binds a society or a family of societies together
over long periods of time. To survive, a civilization needs to have
the means to defend itself, usually military and diplomatic, from
external threats. It needs systems of internal order, usually
defined by customs, laws, and magistrates. Above all it needs
moral and spiritual resources that generate loyalty to recognized
authorities and allow individuals to actualize their full potential
as human beings. The spiritual resources of a civilization provide
those who share them with an identity that transcends the identity belonging to individual peoples united merely by common
descent (the premodern meaning of "nation," *natio* in Latin).
They produce a common culture that may last many centuries
and even outlive the collapse of civilizational order.

All this is rather abstract. We can better understand what a civilization *is* by grasping what it *does*. Consider, then, what it means when we say that someone is civilized. To be civilized, in essence, is to act in ways that make us and those around us better and happier. This is not as straightforward as it may sound. Civilized behavior is more than a matter of having good intentions. It has to be learned, and learning to be civilized requires conscientious effort and practiced judgment. Individuals cannot learn how to be civilized by themselves. They acquire the arts of civilization only by participation in the life of a civilized people. The arts of civilization can be nurtured under the protection of one dominant state, like imperial China or the Roman Empire, or they can be nurtured by a family of states that share a common tradition, like the classical Greek city-states or early modern Europe.

Most of us begin to learn what civilized behavior is from our families. If you have been fortunate enough to be raised in a good family, you will have been taught that there are things you do and things you don't do. Your parents taught you not to be selfish, but to share what you have with your brothers and sisters. They taught you it was right to respect your elders and to be grateful for all they have done for you. You should not get angry and fight with your siblings but settle your differences calmly and consider what is best for everyone. You were taught to do your share of the family's work, to be loyal to family members, and not to criticize them in front of outsiders. You were taught that mistreating people outside your family was wrong. You learned courtesy, good manners, to say "please" and "thank you," and to apologize for bad behavior.

Learning to be civilized starts in the family but continues as you enter more fully into larger communities: those of your school, your religion, your town, and your country. As a representative of your country, you may one day be called upon to act in civilized ways when dealing with other countries. To be civilized you need to know how to treat equals with the respect due to them, to defer to rightful superiors, and to treat those under your authority with fairness and goodwill. You must learn to be a good friend. You must develop a proper sense of who you are – your roots – and what is expected of you as a member of a neighborhood, an institution, or a political community. You should acquire a discriminating enjoyment of literature and the arts that nurtures a deep and sympathetic understanding of your world. You should learn to respect the wisdom of religion. All this will help you to understand people who are different from you and to discover a higher purpose for your life. You should also learn to honor those who have built and defended your civilization, and to preserve the ways of civilized life for later generations.

If we want to be civilized people, we must learn to be proud of the right things in the right way. Those of us who live in Western countries can rightfully be proud of the achievements of our ancestors. Societies belonging to the Western tradition can boast of unsurpassed achievements in music, poetry, imaginative literature, history, architecture, philosophy, and science. But pride in Western achievements should never lead us to despise non-Western societies. Loyalty to our own traditions should not blind us to our own weaknesses or to the achievements of others. A fair-minded student of world civilizations, for example, might easily conclude that imperial China was far more successful at the arts of peaceful government, and over a much longer period, than any society in the Western tradition before modern times. He might judge that Hindu and Buddhist societies produced far richer traditions of moral self-cultivation than any found in the West, or that the rulers of Islamic countries had a more serious public commitment to charity than existed anywhere in premodern Europe. The institution of chattel slavery – treating human beings as private property, subhuman tools of their masters' will – was far more central to the economies of ancient Greece and Rome (and for over two hundred years in parts of the early modern West) than it was in some other historical civilizations. Not all civilizations glorify war to the extent that some Western societies have done.

None of this is to say than non-Western civilizations do not have faults as great or greater than those of the West. The point is not to declare winners and losers in some imaginary competition between world civilizations, but rather to alert us to the pitfalls of civilizational pride. The old moralists distinguished between "proper pride" and sinful pride. Pride in our civilization is a good and necessary thing. It is even, rightly understood, a virtue. The ancient Greek philosopher Aristotle said that human beings have the virtue of proper pride "when they both are and believe themselves to be worthy of great things." They have great souls, *megalopsychia*. But if they believe themselves to be great beyond their actual merits, then they are fools and not virtuous. They suffer from what the Greeks called *hubris*, the delusion that human beings can compete with gods. In the Christian tradition, an exaggerated sense of our own merit is called vanity, and it is a sin. The display of vanity is vainglory, and it is not only sinful, but ridiculous.

As Westerners we learn proper pride when we study the history of our civilization and realize the extraordinary things that our forebears have accomplished. Their achievements can inspire us to admirable deeds in our own life and actions. They elevate our standards. It's like being an athlete who joins a successful team: you have to raise your game. Or you might compare being a proud Westerner to someone who is brought up in an old and famous family. Pride in belonging to that family imposes a sense of duty to live up to its finest traditions.

Proper pride is kept healthy by gratitude, a sense of honor, and a proper humility. Through gratitude we become conscious that our own achievements are not entirely our own: we always stand on the shoulders of giants. Others have worked to make our achievements possible. A sense of honor makes us uphold the best in our traditions: if we want to take pride in them, we cannot bring disgrace on them by bad behavior. We want to be worthy of our inheritance, and we want to be honored by people and institutions that themselves deserve honor.

A proper humility keeps pride from becoming arrogance. Proper humility is the consciousness that we may be worthy of great things, but we are quite capable of doing disgraceful things when tempted or intimidated. If we criticize the greatest men and women of the past, as we sometimes must, our criticism should be tempered by recognition of their greatness and our own smallness. To find fault with extraordinary figures like Pericles, Queen Elizabeth I, or Abraham Lincoln is a bit like spectators at a sporting event or a concert disparaging great athletes or brilliantly talented musicians. Others may ask us – and rightly so! – who are we to be pointing out the faults of others? Have our own actions been so faultless, are our own skills so remarkable, that we can appoint ourselves as judges of the great? We should rather praise and blame our ancestors in a manner that befits our standing as beneficiaries of a great tradition. To do so is *decens*, the Latin word that stands behind the English word "decent." It is seemly or becoming to persons like ourselves; it has a graceful fitness that is constructive and reflects well on us. A proper humility leaves us readier to admire and learn from men and women of great achievement, and slower to think that the present generation is called upon to be the censors of mankind, as many today seem to believe.

In recent times we have seen spread through our schools and institutions an improper and uncivilized humility, a malicious form of humility indistinguishable from self-hatred. This is a humility that humiliates, that seeks to blind Westerners to their magnificent traditions and to rub their noses, like misbehaving dogs, in their worst offenses. The effect if not the goal of this movement of self-humiliation is to make Westerners ashamed of their own civilization and to take away from us the very inheritance that our parents and ancestors worked and fought so hard to hand down to us. It makes us reluctant to add to that inheritance and pass it on to those who will come after us.

These attacks on Western civilization illustrate a sad truth about all civilizations at all times: their fragility. We know of some civilizations, like the gigantic Khmer Empire of medieval southeast Asia, almost as vast as the Roman Empire, which left no literary record at all of its history and culture. Fortunately, a total loss of memory has never happened in Western countries, though the threat of it happening at certain times was real enough. What we call "Western civilization" is actually a succession of civilizations: principally those of the Greeks and the Romans; the Latin and Greek civilizations of medieval Christendom; and the civilization of Europe from the Renaissance down to modern times. In recent centuries European civilization was spread around the world by

European soldiers, colonists, merchants, missionaries, and educators. Today there are fully "Western" countries like Australia and New Zealand in the Pacific Ocean where the dominant population is ethnically European. There are other nations like Japan and India that are not ethnically European but have absorbed certain features of the modern West such as experimental science, parliamentary democracy, or capitalism. Modern Western civilization is a third- or fourth-order civilization that has inherited essential elements of its culture from earlier peoples who lived in no single part of the world.

What binds all these civilizations together, from the Greeks to the modern West, is tradition. Tradition is a word taken from Latin, *traditio*, which literally means "a handing down." There have been moments in the history of the West when the greatest achievements of its predecessor civilizations were in danger of being lost and forgotten. Some of the most famous works of literature and philosophy from ancient Greece and Rome that we still read today barely survived the Middle Ages. For example, in the fourteenth century the complete works of Plato were preserved only in three or four manuscripts; the poetry of Catullus, a number of works by Cicero, and numerous books of Livy, at certain points in their transmission, survived in single manuscripts. Without Cicero or Livy we would know far less about the Roman Republic; without Plato the heights of ancient philosophy would be hidden from our view. These writings and many others were preserved by a handful of devoted scholars, many of them monks, who cared about preserving the literary record of Greco-Roman civilization at times when few others did.

More commonly, however, the arts and sciences of earlier civilizations were preserved by the nations that conquered them.

Instead of wiping out all memory of their enemies, as too often happens in human history, some conquerors were wise enough to recognize and preserve the achievements of the peoples they had defeated in battle. This is what happened when the Romans conquered the eastern Mediterranean in the second century B.C., home to the civilization of the Greeks. Enlightened Romans admired the extraordinary achievements of Greek culture and realized how much they could profit from preserving and adapting them to the needs of Roman society. They began a project lasting many generations to integrate the refined culture of Greece – its arts, literature, science, and philosophy – with Roman military power and statecraft. Rome later created its own great literature, following Greek models. Thus, in the famous words of the Roman poet Horace, "captive Greece took her savage captor captive."

Seventeen centuries later, the few remaining fragments of Hellenic civilization in the eastern Mediterranean were again threatened with extinction, when the last empire of the Greeks, the Byzantine Empire, was crushed by the Ottoman Turks. But the scholars and merchant-princes of the Italian Renaissance, realizing the potential loss to civilization, sent agents to the eastern Mediterranean to collect Greek manuscripts and invite Greek scholars to teach in the West. Over the next century western European scholars printed in Greek and translated into Latin most of the surviving monuments of Greek literature, philosophy, and science. The language of ancient Greece and its literature began to be taught in European schools, alongside Latin literature. Simultaneously, the Roman Church led the effort to preserve the heritage of Greek Christianity in the West. Thanks to these heroic deeds of scholarship, the European Renaissance created a new civilization in which the Greco-Roman inheritance was fused with the legal, scientific, and theological traditions of medieval Christendom. The search for a harmonious and mutually supportive relationship between the classical and Christian elements in the Western tradition, begun already in late antiquity, was to remain a characteristic feature of European civilization down to modern times. Their reconciliation was most nobly expressed in the art of the High Renaissance.

In recent decades, as the classical inheritance has gradually faded from the consciousness of educated people, we sometimes hear the ignorant or tendentious claim that Western civilization is an invented tradition, that "there is no such thing as Western civilization." It is true, to be sure, that the *term* "Western civilization" was hardly used before the twentieth century. It became popular in the era of the two world wars as a way to draw North Americans and overseas Britons closer to Europe and to encourage them to take responsibility for their common heritage. But the *thing* denoted by the term "Western civilization" is, emphatically, no invention. Americans and other Western nations around the globe do in fact share a heritage with European nations that goes back to classical Greece. It permeates the modern West from top to bottom.

The Western tree

What is the Western tradition? One way to describe it is to visualize it as a great tree with a vast root system hidden beneath the surface of the earth. Through historical study we can develop a kind of X-ray vision that helps us to see that system, all but invisible to the uneducated. An educated person understands how the Western tradition draws its nourishment from roots sunk deep through layers of soil and subsoil, down into the bedrock of antiquity.

The taproot of this Western civilizational tree still draws nourishment from the language and literature of classical Greece and Rome. Over 60 percent of English words have Latin or Greek roots, and the percentage is much higher in Italian, Spanish, and French. The technical language of medicine is still based on Greek, and modern legal literature is filled with Latin terms and phrases. Most Western literary genres also have roots in antiquity. The Greeks invented the forms of epic and lyric poetry, elegy, and epigram. Comedy, tragedy, and the novel were also pioneered by the Greeks, satire by the Romans. Narrative history and biography in the West begins with Herodotus and Livy, Thucydides and Tacitus, Plutarch and Suetonius. Western oratory descends from Demosthenes and Cicero, though later times rarely if ever surpassed those great models of noble eloquence.

Western philosophy, particularly its emphasis on argument and proof, goes back to the Greeks of the classical period. Western metaphysics was founded by South Italian Greeks in the fifth century B.C. Socrates inspired many philosophical schools and provided the model for the philosophical life: a life devoted to seeking truth and goodness. Plato and the Stoic philosophers founded ways of thinking about the world and human behavior that gave rise to continuous traditions in the West through the Middle Ages and down to our own times. Aristotle's philosophical works, especially his logical writings, formed the backbone of European university education from the twelfth to the seventeenth century. His moral philosophy is a part of the modern Western canon and is still studied by college students today.

Most of the conclusions of ancient Greek science and medicine were discarded in early modern Europe, but some Greek scientific principles, such as the need for the systematic collection of evidence, remain valid. The Greeks also invented mathematics, and the scientific achievement of the modern West is inconceivable without Plato's intuition that the structure of nature was fundamentally mathematical. Modern technology found inspiration in Archimedes' application of mathematics to problems of engineering and mechanics in the third century B.C.

In the realms of government and law, though modern representative democracy differs from the participatory democracy of ancient Greece, the principle that all citizens should play some part in their own government has inspired Western thinkers and statesmen since the High Middle Ages. The vocabulary and analysis of political stability and change remain heavily dependent on the Greeks, especially Plato and Aristotle, to this day. Republican governments since the Middle Ages have been inspired by Roman models. The most precious principle of modern government, the rule of law – the conviction that the legal system should provide equal justice to all persons, regardless of their power or status – was the creation of Roman jurists. There was a continuous tradition of commentary on Roman law in Western universities from the twelfth to the nineteenth centuries, and Roman principles of public and private law still run in the bloodstream of all Western legal systems today.

In the plastic arts, the classical language of architecture was invented by the Greeks and enhanced and adapted creatively to new purposes by the Romans. It deeply influenced early Christian and Byzantine architecture and experienced several revivals in modern times, beginning with the Renaissance. A splendid revival of classical architecture is occurring once again in our own times. The Western tradition of sculpture also begins with the Greeks and inspired brilliant revivals in the plastic arts of the Renaissance, Baroque, and Neoclassical periods. The painting of the classical world, being physically more fragile, had less influence on later periods, but the few examples that survived, and literary descriptions in ancient authors like the elder Pliny, were foundational. For instance, the ancients' commitment to the representation of nature and to stimulating appropriate emotions in the viewer were primary goals of the visual arts from the late Middle Ages down to modern times.

In the sphere of faith and spirituality, we still live in a world created by ancient religion, and the Roman Catholic Church is the only human institution that has survived continuously from the ancient world into the present. The Christian tradition was formed in the first century A.D., but it built on the much older traditions of Judaism, and it retained the Hebrew Bible as part of its sacred scriptures. Already in the first century it began to interpret its theology in terms drawn from Stoicism and Platonism, and Christianity's dialogue with Greek philosophy continued through the Middle Ages and the early modern period. Christian theology to this day maintains its vitality by returning to the Jewish and Greek sources of its religious vision. The tradition of Biblical commentary has had a continuous history from antiquity to the present.

Many traditions which today are thought to define what it is to be Western in fact have shallower roots in the Western past. The institution of the university, in part indebted to the Islamic *madrasa*, was founded in the late twelfth century, and several great modern universities such as Paris, Oxford, Cambridge, and

Bologna have a continuous history back to that founding period. The gothic style, invented in twelfth-century France, is still being used today, particularly for university buildings. Popular romantic songs and stories of today have roots in the French chivalric literature of the Middle Ages. The legal principle of due process was the invention of thirteenth-century jurists, and the idea that rights inhere in privileged corporations and property-owning individuals was also first explored in medieval courts of law. The practices of consultation that led to representative government can be traced back to European parliaments of the thirteenth century. The establishment in the Middle Ages of a spiritual government independent of lay government, employing a separate legal code (canon law) to regulate the behavior of Christians in their religious life, was invented by the popes of the High Middle Ages. It did not survive the Reformation, but its rejection created a conceptual space (or vacuum) which liberal theorists of the early modern period would define as a space of freedom.

It was only to the early modern period, indeed, that we can trace much of what today is considered characteristically Western. The Western scientific tradition goes back to antiquity, but the modern scientific method – "the discovery of how to discover," the approach to science that has given human beings such power over nature in the last two centuries – first emerged in the seventeenth century. The Western doctrines of natural equality and natural rights, though inspired by Christian theology, also acquired their modern form in the later seventeenth century. The theoretical underpinnings of limited government, toleration, and religious pluralism were a product of the early Enlightenment. The later Enlightenment, in the person of Adam Smith, produced the first powerful arguments in favor of free markets and free trade.

ALLEN C. GUELZO & JAMES HANKINS

Civilization's march

Our march through all these Western traditions since antiquity, rapid though it has been, should expose the naiveté of recent activists who want to uproot Western civilization and replace it with utopias of their own devising. In fact, Western countries can no more cease being Western than an individual can discard his own DNA and choose a new set of genes. Someone who destroys his own DNA would cease to exist; trees that are uprooted die. We are what we are and can only choose to cultivate our sound traditions, to prune away the mistakes of the past, and to repudiate our crimes. We cannot pretend that history did not happen. To condemn the whole Western tradition as "fundamentally flawed," as some do today, is a sign either of colossal ignorance or malicious fanaticism – or both. Some modern critics of the great tree of Western civilization are less radical and would like merely to hack off a few branches here, kill parts of its root system there, replacing these as necessary with artificial roots and branches engineered to modern standards. But these critics are, as a rule, poor political gardeners; they have no deep understanding of how civilizations have been improved in the past, and they are heedless of the ways that civilizations have fallen into ruin. Only the study of history can teach us the best ways to cultivate the garden of civilization, protect it from internal diseases and parasites, and fence it off from external threats.

The greatest threats to Western civilizations before the modern era came from hostile empires – such as the Persian and Parthian Empires of antiquity and the Ottoman Empire of early modern times – as well as from semi-nomadic groups that both Greeks and Romans referred to as barbarians. Barbarism, in fact, is considered the lexical and conceptual opposite of civilization. Historically and etymologically, civilization has been associated with cities. The first were built around six thousand years ago in Mesopotamia and flourished in symbiosis with an agricultural economy. Outside these settled regions with urban centers dwelt nomadic peoples who had no fixed habitation and lived by hunting, foraging wild plants, and finding pasture for livestock. Cities had social hierarchies; nomads were organized more loosely into tribes and clans led by chieftains. Since nomadic life was economically less secure than settled agriculture, nomadic peoples tended to live in a hostile, parasitic relationship with civilized peoples, who clustered in temperate zones and fertile regions able to support large-scale agriculture. Sometimes nomadic peoples organized themselves into powerful armies and were able to overrun civilized parts of the globe, controlling them for their own benefit. Sometimes, as in China, the Mughal Empire of India, and early medieval Europe, barbarian kingships absorbed the cultural heritage of the peoples they defeated and formed hybrid civilizations. In Western lands, barbarian armies were a serious menace to the Roman order from the third century A.D. to the fall of Rome (476 A.D.) and remained threats to the sub-Roman kingdoms of the early medieval West down through the eleventh century.

The Roman Empire, for its part, recognized a duty to civilize the barbarians who came under its rule. In the typical Roman view, the barbarians were impoverished, semi-nomadic peoples living in villages rather than towns. They engaged in incessant warfare as a way of life and had little or no commerce. They spoke myriad ethnic languages that inhibited their participation in the Roman

ALLEN C. GUELZO & JAMES HANKINS

order and kept them from accessing the resources of civilization, its arts and sciences and philosophy. They worshipped strange, bloodthirsty gods and sometimes engaged in human sacrifice. Their way of life, in other words, prevented them from being not just Roman, but fully human. The Romans believed that their state had a duty to bring peace, order, commerce, education, and settled agriculture to barbarian lands. These were the preconditions of civilized life, thanks to which the barbarians would be able to achieve what the civilized world had already achieved: economic security, political integration, and personal moral and spiritual development. Barbarians would thus acquire full *humanitas*, a Latin word that can also be translated as "civilization." Pliny the Elder wrote that through Roman power Italy had become

> the parent of all lands, chosen by the power of the gods to make even heaven more splendid, to gather together the scattered realms and to soften their customs and unite the discordant wild tongues of so many peoples into a common speech, so they might understand each other, and give civilization (*humanitas*) to mankind; in short to become the homeland of every people in the entire world.

It might require coercion to subdue the barbarous, but the belief of the more principled Romans was that subduing the barbarians by force in the short run would enhance their potential for full humanity in the long run. This was the *mission civilisatrice* of imperial Rome, imitated in later times by the Spanish, English, and French Empires – though all too often that mission turned into something hypocritical and corrupt, and was invoked merely to justify outright conquest and exploitative forms of colonialism.

CIVILIZATION & TRADITION

The Romans and later Western imperialists, however, also nurtured certain principles and attitudes that helped them resist the temptation to oppress the barbarian peoples they had conquered, embracing them instead as equally human and even as fellow citizens. One of the virtues of societies belonging to the Western tradition is that they have ordinarily been willing to learn from non-Western societies – not only from advanced societies like the Persians and Chinese but even from peoples they judged to be less civilized. No other world civilization has devoted as much effort to studying other peoples and civilizations, learning their languages and understanding their arts, literature, religion, governments, and culture. Familiarity may sometimes breed contempt, but in general learning about other societies is more likely to lead to respect, even in the case of so-called barbarians. Thus we find the Roman historian Tacitus praising the rustic virtue and courage of Germanic barbarians, inveterate enemies of the Romans, comparing them favorably with the effete, over-civilized Romans of his time. In the Middle Ages, while Christian knights were fighting Islamic armies in the Levant, their brothers back home in French and English universities were reading Muslim philosophical treatises and commentators on Aristotle. Through war and disease the conquering Spaniards of the sixteenth century eliminated large portions of the native populations of the New World, often treating them with sickening cruelty, but they also collected records which they and later scholars have used to reconstruct pre-Columbian civilizations. The same British merchants and administrators who used military force to establish their rule in India during the nineteenth century also collected Indian art, preserved ancient ruins, and studied the written sources of earlier Indian history, founding traditions of scholarship that endure today. Though some modern critics see these studies as just another form of oppression – another way for conquerors to control their subjects – it would be fairer to admit that Western studies of colonized peoples also led to the preservation and learned study of many native cultures that would otherwise have been lost to memory. Today those erudite traditions can provide a basis for mutual understanding between Western countries and their former colonies.

Western ethical traditions also softened the hard edge of imperial dominance. War and conquest often lead combatants to dehumanize their enemy, but Stoic philosophy, which had a quasi-official position in the Roman world, taught that even enemies had to be treated with respect as rational and moral beings. All individuals, civilized or barbarian, belonged to a greater human community: a *cosmopolis*, a world-state visible to the eye of the philosopher. For Cicero, the greatest of Roman orators, all humanity was regulated by the same law of nature, was permeated by the same divine spirit, and therefore constituted, in some larger sense, a community. Though the Stoic doctrine of *oikeosis* (or "appropriation," "endearment") meant that our duties to those closest to us are more primary and generate more direct claims on our benevolence, in principle we have a duty of benevolence to all human beings. The word *humanitas* is also the name of a virtue. A person with the virtue of *humanitas* – a humane warrior or a humane ruler, for example – is one who does not take advantage of his superior power over another person but respects the weaker person's claim on him as a fellow human being.

Christian faith also supported a humane cosmopolitanism. In the New Testament book of Acts (17:26–29) the Apostle Paul, preaching to a pagan audience in Athens – an audience that included Stoic philosophers – asserted a common humanity based on common descent from a single man, Adam, and on a future state of perfect justice that will be brought into the world by the divine man, Jesus Christ. In Paul's vision of the Church, all human beings are equal in the sight of God and all human distinctions of ethnicity or class must disappear. All peoples, whether Jews, Greeks, barbarians, or anyone else, are "fellow citizens with God's people and also members of his household" (Ephesians 2:19). In later periods of Western history Paul's words were regularly taken as prohibiting the enslavement of Christians by Christians. Hence when the Spanish conquered Central and South America in the sixteenth century they were told by religious authorities that they would have to choose between converting the native peoples to Christianity or enslaving them. Of course the behavior of Western peoples all too frequently fell below Paul's high standard of inclusion and humane feeling, but it is a ruinous error of judgment to condemn high principles because the practice of those principles has been flawed.

In recent times the failure of Western nations to live up to their principles has been used to accuse Westerners of hypocrisy or even condemn the Western tradition as a whole. Premodern Westerners, however, were themselves well aware of the yawning gap that could sometimes open between the teachings of their civilization and the behavior of those who called themselves civilized. Already in their classical period the Greeks were asking the question: who are the real barbarians? We Greeks call the Persians barbarians and claim civilization for ourselves, but isn't our own behavior toward each other sometimes far worse than anything the Persians ever did to us? Extreme events such as war, famine, and epidemics could at times remind the Greeks of the barbarism that lay just beneath the surface of their civilization. The greatest historian of antiquity, Thucydides, made it a major theme of his history how the Greeks had barbarized themselves over two decades of warfare, committing unspeakable atrocities against their fellow Greeks. "War is a teacher of violence," he wrote, noting how the Greeks, for all their claims of civility and piety towards the gods, had not hesitated in their warlike rage to slaughter the entire male populations of cities they had conquered and to enslave their women and children. Another Greek writer, Xenophon, a student of Socrates, tried to show his fellow Greeks that the Persians, whom the Greeks labeled barbarians and considered their inferiors, were more wisely governed than they were themselves. In his fictionalized history of Cyrus II, the founder of the Persian Empire, he taught that civilization does not come from membership in a race, but from good customs and good character.

Twenty centuries later, the great French writer Michel de Montaigne in his *Essays* (1580–88) asked Europeans to ponder whether they, the nations of the all-conquering civilization of the West, who had brought a large part of the globe under their sway during the previous century, were in fact barbarians, morally inferior to the savage cannibals they had stumbled across in the jungles of Brazil. To most Europeans the question would have seemed utterly absurd on its face, but Montaigne, in explaining the warrior code that underpinned the rituals of cannibalism, showed Europeans how their own cruel customs of torture, their monstrously inhuman punishments meted out to heretics and criminals, made them far more barbarous than the naked savages of Brazil.

> I am not sorry that we notice the barbarous horror of such acts [cannibalism], but I am heartily sorry that, judging their faults rightly, we should be so blind to our own. I think there is more barbarity in eating a man alive than in eating him dead; and in tearing by tortures and the rack a body still full of feeling, in roasting a man bit by bit, in having him bitten and mangled by dogs and swine (as we have not only read but seen within fresh memory, not among ancient enemies, but among neighbors and fellow citizens, and what is worse, on the pretext of piety and religion), than in roasting and eating him after he is dead.

Montaigne was as civilized a man as Europe could produce in that era: well traveled, deeply learned in Greek and Latin literature, public-spirited, full of humane sympathy and understanding of others, kind, pious, and wise as Socrates. He owed much of this to the civilization that nurtured him, as he acknowledged, but unlike many he also recognized that civilization was a process and not a state. Civilizations could improve, but they could also go bad; they could normalize evil customs and practices that blind us to our own wickedness. From Montaigne we learn that to be civilized does not mean passive acceptance of all received authorities and practices. To remain civilized requires vigilant and lucid appraisal of what we have received, using our full humanity to judge what is truly good and to reject what is corrupt and destructive. Civilization is always threatened by barbarism, and the greater threat often comes more from within than from without. Every man and woman is potentially a person of high cultivation and goodness, but also, potentially, a barbarian.

The test of modernity

By far the greatest achievement of the West, the achievement that has led to its most amazing successes and its most abject failures, was the creation of modernity. Modernity has dramatically changed the life experience of most human beings over the last two centuries. Many historians now believe that the two most fundamental transformations of human life on our planet occurred with the Agricultural Revolution, which began some ten thousand years ago, and the Industrial Revolution that began at the end of the eighteenth century.

The Industrial Revolution is an inadequate name for the comprehensive changes wrought in the way human beings think and live that were brought about chiefly (but not only) by extraordinary advances in science and technology. It is, nevertheless, in the economic life of the human race that the difference modernity makes is most evident to the eye of the historian. Before the Industrial Revolution took hold in the West, most of the human race, including most Westerners, lived at the subsistence level. Mere survival was difficult for the vast majority of people, and overall life expectancy was low. Scarce resources made premodern peoples readier to go to war, readier to rebel against their rulers, readier to persecute others, and readier to immigrate to new lands when life became precarious.

Around the end of the eighteenth century, a dramatic change began in the human condition that historians have dubbed "the

Great Enrichment." The average income of Europeans began to increase rapidly. It doubled, then doubled again. It continued to double every generation down through the twentieth century. The massive increase in the wealth of Western societies over two hundred years went together with other unprecedented changes. Life expectancy has more than doubled. Urbanization, which had been increasing gradually for thousands of years, exploded. Enormous concentrations of capital began to appear, which fed astonishing technological advances. In 1903, the first motor-powered aircraft was invented; in 1969, the first humans landed on the moon.

No reasonable person would think of rejecting the real benefits of modernity. But modernity has also given rise to a mentality or way of thinking, called "modernism" here, whose effects on our civilization have been far from benign. The enormous advances in material life experienced by Western and Westernized nations in the last two centuries have given the modernist mentality great power over the minds of intellectuals and revolutionaries. In its most militant forms that power has even been used intentionally to destroy civilizations. It has brought untold suffering and death to tens of millions across the globe, betraying the promise of modernity itself.

At the center of the modernist mentality is a model of historical development known as the "idea of progress." Western literati going back to antiquity had always acknowledged that human beings could and in fact had improved their lot through science and technology, and that civilized life could and in fact had spread widely. They were also well aware that civilization was fragile, empires rose and fell, and that human advances could be abused or forgotten. But from the later eighteenth century onwards many thoughtful persons – as was natural for people living through the Great Enrichment – began to believe that human progress was inevitable so long as traditional authorities were dethroned and Science – with a capital "S" – raised up in their place. The civilized traditions of the past must be discarded, they believed, if the ideal futures men were beginning to imagine for themselves were to be fulfilled.

The creators of the idea of progress, who belonged to the movement known as the Enlightenment, also praised freedom as progress's necessary condition. This did much to establish a presumption in favor of political liberty, freedom of religion, and human rights. Rightly understood and rightly ordered, these principles can and do contribute to the betterment of mankind. But the creators of the myth of progress also helped create a politics and a rhetoric of progress that defined progress as material abundance, as ever-increasing autonomy of the individual from society, and as a license to transcend the limits of human nature.

It was this modernist narrative that gave sanction to the worst excesses of totalitarian governments in modern times. The idea of progress as weaponized by modernists has crippled the ability of our Western traditions to perform their proper functions: to anchor us in the past, to engender noble aspirations, and to foster in us reverence for our forebears and for established authorities.

Some recent thinkers have argued that the only way to save modernity is to free it of militant modernism. A culture that cannot balance the modern and the traditional, one that is all for the modern and all against the traditional, will end up destroying itself. When the moral capital of Western civilization is finally exhausted, we will not have entered some brave new world. We will have compassed our own destruction. What the barbarian hordes of ancient and medieval times were unable to accomplish, we will have done to ourselves.

This, indeed, is the great test that Western civilization faces in our time. We need to find a new balance between tradition and innovation, to modernize with moderation, without losing that inheritance of immeasurable value that we call the Western tradition. The great British statesman Edmund Burke, in 1790, on the very brink of modernity, wrote: "People will not look forward to posterity who never look backwards to their ancestors." We too, as people who aspire to civility – to the goodness, truth, and beauty that our tradition, like a river, bears down to us from the civilizations of the past – have a duty to study and cherish what we have been given by our ancestors, and to preserve it for our children.

A Popular Form of Monomania

ANTHONY DANIELS

*"We hope by this time next year to have from a hundred and
fifty to two hundred healthy families cultivating coffee
and educating the natives of Borrioboola-Gha,
on the left bank of the Niger."*

MRS. JELLYBY
Bleak House, by Charles Dickens (1852)

CONCEPTIONS OF MORALITY change, never more so than in
the lifetime of *The New Criterion*. If a person who died at the
time of the first issue were to return to life, he would find himself
in an angrier and more charged moral atmosphere than the one
he had left – and one in which the principles that undergird
Western civilization scarcely seem to be in evidence. Indeed, he
would think that the world was a moral hornets' nest that had
been poked with a stick, so furious is the buzzing.

Some years ago, I shared a public platform with a person considerably more eminent than I. The subject of discussion was
what it took to be good, which can be argued over for an eternity
without compelling a universally accepted answer. This does not
make the question meaningless, however, as the Logical Positiv-
ists might once have claimed; indeed, there are few questions
more important.

A POPULAR FORM OF MONOMANIA

The person more eminent than I (whom I shall not name, the avoidance of pointless personal denigration being a part, albeit a small one, of what it takes to be good) said that it took intelligence to be good. Since the eminent person almost certainly considered only the upper 1 or 2 percent of the population to be intelligent, and since he claimed that intelligence was a necessary but not sufficient condition of goodness, it was clear that he did not think much of the moral qualities of the great majority of his fellow creatures. His answer was perfectly compatible with the claim that only one in a thousand people is good.

I said that I thought that what he said was appalling, true neither philosophically nor empirically. But just because a viewpoint is bad philosophically, is empirically without foundation, horrible in its implications, does not mean that it cannot be held. History would no doubt have been rather different if this had been impossible.

It is always a good idea to try to elucidate what can be said in favor of an opinion with which you disagree: there is probably no better way of getting one's own thoughts clear. What, then, can be said in favor of the idea that one must be clever to be good?

There must surely be some cognitive element to goodness; one does not speak of a morally good bird or lizard, for example. And if to be good means a disposition to be good and not merely to perform an occasional good act, as if almost by chance, then cognition clearly has a part to play in being good. Cognitive ability – intelligence – should therefore be at least an advantage in, if not actually a precondition of, being good.

This is all the more so since moral decisions are often complex rather than simple and straightforward. The world is not so constituted that it only provides us with easy moral questions to answer, which is why laying down invariable moral rules is so difficult. Circumstances really do alter cases; if they did not, Kant's view that we should tell the truth even to a murderer on his way to cut someone's throat, simply because we should always tell the truth, would not strike us as so absurd, believable only for a man with little ordinary intercourse with the world.

When to speak the truth, when to hold one's tongue, when to indulge in euphemistic evasion, when to tell little white lies for the good of others – these are subtle questions often requiring a swift appreciation of the many possible reasons or circumstances that must go toward sound judgment. Surely high intelligence, in the meaning of my co-panelist, helps here?

But whether or not it does so cannot be answered in *a priori* fashion. Even if *some* intelligence were required to be good, the relationship, if any, between its level and goodness would still have to be established. It might well be, for example, that there is an adequate level of intelligence above which any surplus contributes nothing as far as moral character is concerned. I think this is ordinarily the case: we do not expect better behavior of someone with an IQ of 140 than of someone with an IQ of 110. And if the man with the higher intelligence quotient is bad, he is probably better at being bad.

Understanding the moral argument for a certain course of action is not the same as performing that action: indeed, most of humanity has found the former rather easier than the latter. I once worked in a prison as a doctor, and though the prisoners were, on the whole, poorly educated, and though it is generally held that prisoners are of a lower average or median intelligence than that of the general population, I found that very few of them were moral imbeciles in the sense that they could not understand or grasp a moral argument. Clearly, many of them had difficulty in applying the conclusion of that argument in practice, but their problem was not with intelligence.

It is in any case a matter of common experience that the best people one knows are not necessarily the most intelligent – though I do not want to imply, either, that high intelligence is incompatible with goodness. In fact, in my experience there is little or no relation between goodness and intelligence.

Why, then, did my co-panelist, himself highly intelligent, assert something so patently false? I think it was because there has been a progressive distancing of the locus of moral concern, at least among the educated, from personal conduct to wider, impersonal questions.

This is not an entirely new phenomenon. Lenin, for example, wrote that "our [Bolshevik] morality is entirely subordinated to the interests of the class struggle of the proletariat." All other morality, according to Lenin, was deception and dupery, designed to throw dust in the proletariat's eyes. He, at any rate, found his theory of morality extremely liberating: since it was he who decided what was in the interests of the class struggle of the proletariat, it meant that he could do what he liked. And what he liked, often enough, was to have priests, poets, and sundry other enemies murdered.

In similar fashion, Islamists think that whatever supposedly defends or advances their brand of Islam is both morally justified and obligatory, making irrelevant all other considerations that are normally thought to be moral. This, too, liberates them from restraint, though not necessarily to the direct personal advantage of those who act in accord with the doctrine – unless, that is, they really *are* rewarded in heaven.

Leninism and violent Islamism are, of course, extreme examples of what happens when a narrow ideology is made the philosophical basis of moral action. Such ideologies are not founded and propagated by men lacking in intelligence, though their rank-and-file followers may well be of lesser intelligence than they. Lenin, surely one of the most unattractive figures in world history though for decades treated in the Soviet Union as a moral exemplar, the Muhammad of Communism as it were, was certainly not of deficient intelligence. These totalizing ideologies elevate highly doubtful intellectual constructions and abstractions into realities in the mind of the believer, who then views the whole world in their light. The abstractions become more real to believers than the everyday reality in which most of us live most of the time. By this means, viciousness is transmuted into duty and cruelty into an act of cleansing. Sadism is part of the makeup of many people, if not quite of all, and totalizing ideologies appeal to the most sadistic among us, with their justification for, indeed requirement of, conduct that would otherwise be deemed beyond the pale.

Thus intellectualization of a certain kind can promote the dulling of normal moral sensibilities. Even more than political language (as analyzed in Orwell's essay), ideology is designed to make lies sound truthful and murder respectable, indeed to make lies the proclaimed truth from which all dissent is impermissible, and murder a duty.

A POPULAR FORM OF MONOMANIA

Foolishness

It would be an exaggeration to claim that the populations of Western liberal democracies have succumbed entirely to the siren song of totalizing ideologies, but nevertheless the signs are not altogether encouraging. Two factors promote the advance of ideology in our societies: first, the death of God, and second, the spread of tertiary education. The two may well, of course, be related.

Whatever else the death of God may have done for us, it has not lessened our desire for an overall or transcendent meaning or purpose in our lives, especially in conditions in which our basic material needs – those which, when not met, lead to a struggle for existence in the most literal sense – are almost guaranteed to be supplied. This is especially true of those who have been most stimulated to experience the desire for transcendent meaning or purpose, that is to say the educated, by whom I mean those who have passed the first quarter of their lives (at least) in supposedly educational institutions.

In the absence of religious belief – and I take it as axiomatic that religious belief in any other than an etiolated, semi-pagan claim to spirituality is unlikely now to revive with sufficient vigor or unity fundamentally to alter the moral atmosphere, especially in that part of the population that experiences most acutely a need for transcendence – there are relatively few possible sources of meaning greater than that of the flux of everyday life. Chief among these is political ideology, the most obvious being fascism and Marxism. Both have lost their salience for most people, however, fascism because of the appalling catastrophe of Nazism, and Marxism because of its prolonged and brutal failure in Russia.

(However much Marxists proclaimed their distance from the Soviet Union, the ignominious collapse of the Soviet Union profoundly damaged the intellectual prestige of Marxism.)

But just as the death of God did not destroy the human need for transcendence, so the disasters of Nazism and Communism did not halt the search for transcendence by means of ideology. Instead of disappearing, therefore, as one might have expected or at least hoped, ideology in the sense of an overarching system of thought that simultaneously explains the woes of the world and suggests a means to eliminate them, thereby endowing a profound meaning to a person's existence, giving him a cause that appears larger than himself, did not disappear, but on the contrary has flourished *pari passu* with the expansion in tertiary education. This time, ideology appears in a balkanized form, with a rich variety of monomanias, ranging from the "liberation" of sexual proclivities to the salvation of the biosphere. But, as if to prove the theory of intersectionality, various monomanias have formed tactical alliances with one another, such that if you know a person's monomania, you also know what his attitude to many seemingly unrelated questions will be. There has developed a popular front, so to speak, of monomaniacs.

It is not surprising, then, that one's opinion on matters social and political has become for a considerable part of the population the measure of virtue. If you have the right opinions you are good; if you have the wrong ones you are bad. Nuance itself becomes suspect, as it is in a tabloid newspaper, for doubt is treachery and nuance is the means by which bad opinions make their comeback. In this atmosphere, people of differing opinions find it difficult to tolerate each other's presence in a room: the only way to avoid open conflict is either to avoid certain persons or certain subjects. Where opinion is virtue, disagreement amounts to accusation of vice.

Since there is no new thing under the sun, at least where human error and foolishness are concerned, this is far from the first time in history that people have taken opinion as a metonym for virtue. And where there is political divergence, there is the possibility, or likelihood, of polarization, for Man is a dichotomizing animal. Neutrality in a polarized situation is deemed cowardice or betrayal; it is impermissible to have no opinion on an issue, no matter how ill-informed on, or indifferent to, it one might be. The right of non-participation on one side of a debate is abrogated: as some members of the Black Lives Matter movement put it, "silence is violence."

But while polarization of opinion is nothing new, the number of people who concern themselves with political and social affairs in both a theoretical and practical way has increased enormously, and with it the sensation of living amid conflict even in times of peace. Family and generational estrangements on the grounds of opinion, while not unknown previously, have become more common, almost expected. I know of several parents who have to hold their tongues if they wish to maintain relations with their children. No lyricist would now write, as did W. S. Gilbert in 1882,

> I often think it's comical
> How Nature always does contrive
>   That every boy and every gal
>   That's born into the world alive
> Is either a little Liberal
> Or else a little Conservative!

Such lightheartedness is not possible where opinion is the main, or sole, test of decency, the litmus of vice and virtue. Every difference of opinion is a difference not on the single point at issue alone, but of an entire *Weltanschauung*, and a few words are often sufficient to demonstrate which camp a person is in, that of vice or that of virtue.

The extreme importance now given to opinion (by contrast with conduct) in the estimation of a person's character has certain consequences. This is not to say that in the past a person's opinions played no part in such an assessment, and no doubt there are some opinions so extreme or vicious, for example that some whole population should be mercilessly wiped out, that in any day and age one would hesitate to associate with someone who held them. But before, even when someone held an opinion that we considered very bad, we still also assessed the degree of seriousness with which he held it, the degree to which it was purely theoretical, the importance it played in his overall mental life. The holding of such an opinion would not redound to his credit, but if lightly held and with no likely effect on his actual behavior, it would detract only slightly from our view of him. He might still be a good man, albeit one with a quirk, a mental blind spot.

If we take as an example the question of capital punishment, it should be possible for people to disagree without concluding that those who take a different view from their own are morally deficient or defective. I am against the penalty on the grounds that even in the most scrupulous jurisdictions mistakes are made, and that for the state wrongly to execute one of its citizens is a heinous thing, moreover one which will bring the whole criminal justice system into disrepute. If it is argued that the state's unwillingness occasionally to execute wrongfully will lead to more wrongful deaths by murder than would otherwise have occurred, I would reply that this is a price that must be paid (though I concede that there might in theory be a price *too* high to be paid, though I think this is unlikely in practice ever to eventuate). A person who declared himself in favor of summary execution without trial of all those with whom he disagreed or otherwise reprehended would probably be regarded as mad rather than bad, at least outside the purlieus of the Taliban.

If someone were either for or against the penalty on more deontological grounds, that it was either just or barbaric in itself, I would recognize these as sensible arguments without necessarily subscribing to either, and without giving to them the weight that those who subscribe to them give them. Thus, it should be possible for us to have a discussion on the question, disagreeing but without casting aspersions on each other's character. It seems to me, however (though I have no strict scientific evidence to prove it) that such reasonable discussions have become less and less frequent, precisely because opinion and not conduct has become the touchstone of virtue.

This naturally raises the temperature of any discussion and inclines participants to bad temper. But there are other consequences too.

For one thing, the elevation of the moral importance of opinion changes the locus of a person's moral concern from that over which he has most control, namely how he behaves himself, to that over which he has almost no personal control. He becomes a Mrs. Jellyby who, it will be remembered, was extremely concerned about the fate of children thousands of miles away in Africa but completely neglected her own children right under her own eyes, in her house in London.

Opinion & virtue

This is not to say that huge abstract questions, such as the best economic or foreign policy to follow, have no moral content. Of course they do, but generally in a rather vague, diluted, and distant way, for example that one should choose the policy that does the most good or, more realistically, the least harm. This policy is likely to remain extremely difficult to determine, being subject to so many variables. Again, reasonable people are likely to disagree, all the more so as the desiderata of human existence are plural: there is, in most situations other than total war, no one goal that morally trumps all others. If it could be shown that the creation of wealth is favored by, or even requires, a degree of unemployment, but it also accepted that wealth is a good and unemployment is a harm, then decent people might well disagree how much wealth creation should be foregone in order to reduce unemployment, in part because goods and harms are often not commensurable.

The question of what conduces to economic prosperity is large and important, but people may disagree as to the worth – the human worth, that is – of prosperity itself, at least within quite wide limits. But even if they agree as to its worth, and assuming that there is a single indubitable measure of such prosperity, they may still disagree as to how it is to be produced or encouraged. If someone says that personal freedom is a precondition of prosperity, someone else might point to the case of China, whose rise to prosperity has probably been the most remarkable, at least in terms of timescale, in the whole history of the world. China, of course, is a highly authoritarian country. But the first might reply that China in certain respects allows more freedom than Western countries, for the weight of the state in China, so much heavier in some respects than elsewhere, is so much lighter in others. There is no social security there to speak of, so that people must fend for themselves when necessary, and this in turn means that the state is spared the need to raise taxes to pay for social security. Since taxes are generally coerced even in democracies (where one group coerces them from another, and few people pay them if avoidance is possible), there is less coercion in this respect in China than in almost any Western country. Thus is the argument saved that personal freedom is a precondition of prosperity.

It is evident that discussions of this nature can be, and often are, endless: even that of free trade versus protection is not decided once and for all. People engaged upon such debates will rely on what I hesitate to call alternative facts. If there is a correct answer to be had, it cannot be decided by moral virtues of the disputants. The better person may have the worse arguments, and the worse person the better. The difference between *laissez-faire* and *dirigisme* cannot be settled by reference to the moral qualities of those who advocate for either, at least not in a world in which rational argument counts for something.

The overemphasis on opinion as the main or only determinant of a person's moral character thus has the effect of promoting irrationalism, and all argument becomes in effect ad hominem. If a person holds one opinion, he is good; if another, he is bad. Everything is decided in advance by means of moral dichotomy. Nuance disappears. If a person approves of abortion, even in restricted circumstances, he is, for opponents, virtually a child-murderer, and therefore beyond the moral pale. If he does not, he is, for opponents, a misogynist who would condemn girls of twelve to bear the children of their rapists, and therefore beyond the moral pale. One does not willingly talk to or otherwise consort with people beyond the moral pale.

There is a positive-feedback mechanism built into opinion as the measure of virtue, for if it is virtuous to espouse a particular opinion, it is even more virtuous to espouse a more extreme or generalized version of it. It then becomes morally impermissible for a person to hold the relatively moderate opinion; he is denounced with the peculiar venom that the orthodox reserve for heretics. When J. K. Rowling, a feminist once in good odor with the morally self-anointed, delivered herself of an opinion couched in moderate terms stating something so obvious that it will one day (I hope) astonish future social or cultural historians that it needed saying at all, namely that a transsexual woman is not a woman *simpliciter*, she was turned upon viciously, including by those who owed their great fortunes to her – or at least to her work. She had committed the cardinal sin in a world of opinion as the criterion of virtue of not having realized that the moral caravan had moved on. How easily sheep become goats!

Taking opinion as the hallmark of virtue has other effects besides provoking dichotomization, bad temper, and the exertion of a ratchet effect in the direction of ever more extreme and absurd ideas. It tends to limit the imagination, moral and otherwise. For example, once something tangible is declared to be a human right, which no decent person can thenceforth question or deny on pain of excommunication by the virtuous, the good procured by the exercise of that right ceases to be a good for any other reason than that it is a right. The recipient has no reason to feel grateful for what he receives, because it was his right to receive it, though he may, of course, feel rightfully aggrieved if he does *not* receive it. A United Nations *rapporteur* recently condemned New Zealand for its breach of human rights because it did not provide decent housing for all its citizens (and other inhabitants); rents were expensive and there was overcrowding as well as some homelessness. The New Zealand government, which had committed itself to the view that there was a human right to decent housing, meekly promised to try to do better. It had not promised to treat housing *as if* it were a human right, but to treat it as a right itself; it was therefore skewered by its own supposed virtue.

If anyone were to deny that decent housing was a right, it is almost certain that he would soon be attacked as a landlords' apologist, as someone indifferent to the plight of the homeless – as if there could be no other reason why people should be decently housed and not homeless *other* than that they had a human right to decent housing.

The potential consequences of a right to decent housing, if taken seriously, are pretty obvious: the commandeering of private property, for example, which proved such a triumphant success in the Soviet Union that people were living in communal apartments two-thirds of a century later. And since "decency" in housing is not a natural quality but varies according to circumstance (what is verging on the indecent in Auckland, Christchurch, or Wellington would be palatial in Lagos or Dhaka), compliance with such a right is an invitation to, or would require and justify, ceaseless and constant bureaucratic interference. Furthermore, declaring decent housing to be a right, irrespective of the conduct of the person exercising it, would not exactly be a spur to personal effort, especially in the lower reaches of society. And if decent housing is a right, why bother to seek the true economic or social reasons for high rents and homelessness? A right is a right, independent of economics; all that is required is that it be complied with.

These rather obvious objections to the concept of decent housing as a human right are seldom aired, at least in public discussions, because those who make them are so easily portrayed as Gradgrinds or Scrooges, heartless and cruel, lacking in the imagination necessary to understand or sympathize with poverty. The supposed moral quality of the objector trumps the possible validity of his objections, which therefore do not have to be considered. Far from the objector lacking imagination, however, it is the proponent of the human right who lacks it: he fails even to try to imagine what the consequences of what he advocates might be. Words are the money of fools, no doubt, but also of people who desire unlimited powers of interference in the lives of others.

The importance accorded to opinion – correct opinion, of course – as the criterion of virtue has another strange effect, besides increasing intolerance and limiting imagination, for it conduces both to a new dictatorial puritanism and a new libertinism whose equilibrium is forever unstable.

The puritanism manifests itself in language. In the modern moral climate, for example, it is essential to be a feminist. A person who declared himself indifferent, let alone openly hostile, to feminism would be considered by many to be, *ex officio*, a morally depraved person, perhaps even a potential Bluebeard. Purity is imposed on language itself: in Britain, a person who subscribes to "correct" opinion would now not dream of using the word "actress," as it is allegedly demeaning to females who act, suggesting inferiority to (rather than mere sexual difference from) males who act. In France the same type of person would not now dream of using the word *"écrivain"* for a female who writes, instead employing the feminine neologism *"écrivaine,"* because not to do so would imply that writers, at least ones worthy of notice, are solely or predominantly male.

It is obvious from these examples, which demand the defeminization of language on the one hand and its feminization on the other, that the purpose of this language reform is the exercise of power to impose virtue, rather than the solution to any real problem, since neither "actress" nor *"écrivain"* as applied to a woman has intrinsic derogatory connotations.

In similar fashion, American academic books now routinely use the impersonal "she" rather than "he," and sub-editors impose this usage on their authors, even on those women to whom it would not come naturally because of their age. Sometimes such absurdities as alternating the impersonal "he" and "she" are employed, to ensure (or rather imply a deep commitment to) sexual equality; the phrase "she and he" is also employed rather than "he and she," considerations of euphony being disregarded in favor of an ideological commitment to righting past wrongs and protecting women from domestic violence by means of sub-editorial vigilance. No doubt the guardians of "correct" usage imagine that they are doing what would once have been called "God's work," and therefore brook no demurral from their edicts. The mills of the new morality grind very fine indeed.

The new morality

This new morality contrives to be both liberal and illiberal at the same time. It takes as its basic or founding text the famous words of John Stuart Mill in his essay *On Liberty* (1859):

[T]he sole end for which mankind are warranted, individually or collectively, in interfering with the liberty of action of any of their number, is self-protection.... [T]he only purpose for which power can be rightfully exercised over any member of a civilised community, against his will, is to prevent harm to others. His own good, either physical or moral, is not a sufficient warrant.... The only part of the conduct of any one, for which he is amenable to society, is that which concerns others.

Whether or not people have actually read *On Liberty*, Mill has probably had a more profound effect on common modes of political thought than any philosopher other than Marx. Mill's "one very simple principle," as he calls it, is as omnipresent in our way of thinking about morality as the Sermon on the Mount once was.

But the one very simple principle turns out not to be so very simple after all. What seems initially to be permissive, and indeed is used to justify permissiveness, can also be highly restrictive, even totalitarian, in its implications. In the first place, it must meet what might be called the "no-man-is-an-island" objection: human beings are social and political by nature, so that it is difficult to think of any conduct which does not concern others. Even an anchorite who lives in a cave must have cut himself off from people who once knew him, who might be severely affected emotionally by his withdrawal from society. Most of us are very far from being anchorites.

What is less frequently remarked in objection to the very simple principle is that the notion of harm to others is indefinitely expansible. When Mill wrote, life for most people was extremely tough; there was no treatment for most illnesses, and existence therefore hung by a thread, even for the privileged (the life expectancy of members of the British royal family in the middle of the nineteenth century was about forty-five). The slightest injury could, through septicemia, lead quickly to death. In these circumstances, people were likely to take less seriously claims of harm done to themselves by minor inconveniences or verbal infelicities. Real victims were too numerous for claims to victimhood by the objectively fortunate to be entertained with the reverence they now frequently receive. Even in my childhood, we used frequently to recite the old proverb in response to an intended insult, "Sticks and stones may break my bones, but words will never hurt me." No more: in a world in which opinion is the measure of Man, words are poison, dagger, Kalashnikov, hand grenade, and atomic bomb, and no one now gains a reputation for moral uprightness who does not sift the words of others for the wickedness they may contain.

No one could possibly deny the great importance of words and opinions in human life, of course, or their power to give offense and even to provoke violence. Words and opinions may inspire people either to the best or the worst acts, but we do not usually absolve people of their responsibility, or fail to praise or blame them, on the grounds that they were inspired or influenced by the words of others. If I translate your words into deeds (excepting situations of duress or some other extenuating or excusing condition), the responsibility is mine. In advocating the most complete freedom of speech – at least for members of a civilized community who are capable of exercising it, another somewhat fluid and contestable limiting condition – Mill assumed that there was a great gulf fixed between words and opinions on the one hand and deeds on the other.

But now, for the first time, we have found a way to reconcile the most illiberal impulses (and we ought to remember that it does not come naturally to people to grant liberty to others) with Mill's one simple principle, which has achieved almost sacred status and cannot be directly opposed or contradicted head-on. Mill tells us that we must not forbid ourselves anything except that which harms others, but (unlike him) today we have expanded the possible harms to include almost everything that we can say, since offense is harm done to the person who takes offense and there is almost no opinion about anything that might not offend someone. Moreover, taking offense can become a habit, a duty, and a pleasure. Where opinion is virtue, the strength of offense taken is a sign of commitment to virtue, which then sets up a type of arms race of moral exhibitionism, in which my offense taken at something must be greater than yours because only thus can I prove my moral superiority over you. Shrillness then becomes a token of depth of feeling, and no one can feel anything who does not parade his outrage in public.

As with most principles, however, the one which makes everything permissible that does not harm others but which also expands harms to the giving of offense is not applied consistently, to say the least. Only offense against those who hold morally approved ideas counts as harm; offending those who hold disapproved ideas is almost a positive duty. No one, as far as I know, has ever proposed a "safe space" to protect believers from the distress occasioned by reading, say, Hume's *Dialogues Concerning Natural Religion* (1779). As for the protection from taking offense accorded to Muslims, it is (if I may so put it) liberally admixed with fear – but that is another question.

A POPULAR FORM OF MONOMANIA

It is the inconsistency with which the principle is applied that permits or encourages the coexistence of puritanism with libertinism. If we take some sexual proclivity, for example, that previously, and maybe for centuries, was regarded as disgusting or immoral, the liberal discovery that it is perfectly in accordance with morality because it does no harm to anyone who does not refuse consent to it is soon trumpeted as a triumph of liberation; as if to make up for lost time, it soon becomes *de rigueur* not merely to permit what was previously forbidden, but to "celebrate" it. The hidden becomes ubiquitous and the unnameable present on everyone's lips. As readers of Richard von Krafft-Ebing and Havelock Ellis will appreciate, the scope for reform in the direction of public tolerance, to be brought about by righteous agitation, is almost endless. No person for whom opinion is the beginning and end of virtue, and for whom agitation for reform is the *summum* of the good life, need experience the despair expressed by Mill in his moving *Autobiography* (1873) when he asked himself:

> "Suppose that all your objects in life were realized; that all the changes in institutions and opinions which you are looking forward to, could be completely effected at this very instant: would this be a great joy and happiness to you?" And an irrepressible self-consciousness distinctly answered, "No!" At this, my heart sank within me: the whole foundation on which my life was constructed fell down. All my happiness was to have been found in the continual pursuit of this end. The end had ceased to charm, and how could there ever again be any interest in the means? I seemed to have nothing left to live for.

These are thoughts that the modern followers of Mill spare themselves, or perhaps that never occur to them (Mill was, after all, a brilliant man, which many of his modern followers are not). And provided that these thoughts can be kept at bay, the pursuit of various reforms of "institutions and opinions" can give a sense of purpose to a life, deeper currents of human existence being disregarded.

This is not, of course, a plea for immobilism: the need for reform is pretty constant (even if the failure to recognize its potential ill-effects is also pretty constant), and sometimes it is as well that there are persons who make such reform the focus of their lives. William Wilberforce, for example, made the abolition of slavery the aim of his life, and he is rightly honored for it. Furthermore, it is as well that our societies should contain untold numbers of people with like consuming aims: from the search for a cure of a rare metabolic disease to the origins of the Amharic alphabet. The danger comes when the most dubious, even fatuous, social theories and reforms in the name of virtue become the cynosure of the moral life of a large and influential sector of society, namely the intelligentsia that is ultimately the determinant of a modern society's history. This is so even, or perhaps especially, when the intelligentsia in question is ignorant, foolish, grasping, power-hungry, and unrealistic.

The effect, if not the purpose, of the overemphasis on opinion as the whole of virtue is both to liberate and to control. The liberation – from restraint on personal conduct – is for the persons with the right opinions; the control is for, and over, the rest of society. The intelligentsia is thus like an aristocracy, but without the *noblesse oblige* or the good taste that to some extent justified the aristocracy.

Perhaps the most striking illustration of this is the fate of the "revolution" of May 1968: those who wanted to forbid forbidding soon found themselves in control of a state that forbade more than ever, and which insinuated itself by regulation and the passage of myriad laws ever more termite-like into the lives of its citizens, while at the same time allowing for a limited libertinism. As Aldous Huxley said in 1948 in his preface to the second edition of *Brave New World* (to which, incidentally, his own attitude was far more ambivalent than we might suppose), a future government intent on establishing tyrannical control over its population would be advised to grant it freedom in the matter of sex and drugs. *Voilà!* But in the end, the impulse to control is paramount.

The Specter of Chinese Civilization

ANGELO M. CODEVILLA

SINCE FEW DOUBT that the increasingly numerous Chinese people are rising in power and self-confidence while we Americans continue to become less and less attached to the values of our own civilization, it makes some sense to ask whether we are doomed to succumb to Chinese civilization. This is especially pertinent given that the way Chinese people live has always been much the opposite of the way Americans want to live.

Does China represent the fatal crossroads of Western civilization? The question, as phrased, calls for an unequivocal *no*. Americans may well end up living under tyranny resembling that of today's China. But that tyranny's core is not the classic civilization of Confucius, Laozi, and the *Romance of the Three Kingdoms*. This civilization is what the Chinese themselves abandoned around the turn of the twentieth century. Today's tyranny in China itself is by, of, and for the Communist Party. It is Western civilization's perverted legacy, built upon ancestral Chinese habits.

China has not historically been a nursery, never mind an exporter, of totalitarianism or revolution. Moreover, China's rulers have traditionally had neither interest nor capacity to export any way of life. Their goal vis-à-vis America is now to maximize revenue while minimizing America's will and capacity to interfere with China's growing overlordship of Asia. This requires merely co-opting the U.S. ruling class, which the Chinese find easy through garden-variety corruption.

Our own civilization is in the process of being undercut by its own ruling class, which abandoned Western culture as it was taking power over the past century. By then negating explicitly the civilization's defining premise – that all humans are created equally in God's image, and hence that legitimate rule must be based on persuasion rather than force – our ruling class has placed itself on essentially the same ground as that of yesteryear's and today's Chinese despots.

The "Chinese Model" that our side's would-be tyrants are eager to copy merely adds technical refinements to standard despotism. Our leaders want to impose it, confident that Westerners will accept it as the Chinese people do. But they mistake Chinese civilization as well as their own. What they wish to impose is, in fact, different from what exists in China in purpose and nature. Applied in today's Western world for the purposes of our own woke tyranny, Chinese-level social control would be harsher than the Chinese original. Chinese despots offer a calm, orderly tyranny in exchange for equal obedience by all alike. By contrast, our own ruling class demands that one class of people obey another's ever-evolving and unpredictable orders, while submitting to insult and injury. China is not what Americans should fear. Today, as in Lincoln's time, "if destruction be our lot, we must ourselves be its author and finisher."

Totalitarianism is not Chinese

China was never the land of the free. The net of waterworks that irrigated some of the world's most fertile land and facilitated travel within it was the doing of millions of human beings forced to dig. Even the Han Dynasty's hundreds of miles of rammed-earth walls, never mind the later thousands of miles of sculpted stone, bespeak millions worked to death. Emperors and would-be emperors advertised their brutality. Some had themselves depicted wearing robes onto which are embroidered images of bloody heads severed by bloody blades. The Forbidden City's sculptures feature angry, jealous lions and dragons. The emperors' – and their favorites' – choice of everything, including concubines, was arbitrary and absolute.

And yet, law ruled in China. It was not statutory law, never mind natural law. It was customary law, enforced by officials whose expertise in it was certified by rigorous, competitive, high-stakes examinations. Ordinary Chinese depended on that law and its impartial enforcement for the most important things: the duties of children to parents, marriages, titles to land, rents, loans, inheritances, lawsuits, etc. The near-static nature of the supply of land and food, coupled with the constant increase in the population, meant that legal processes secured the livelihood of the most able and doomed the less able to marginalization at best. For millennia, China was the land of law.

The law's content simply reflected how things were done. Things should be done the way they were done, period. Readers of Confucius's *Analects* (*ca.* 475 B.C.–220 A.D.) have always noted their substantive commonality with Aristotle's *Nicomachean Ethics* (*ca.* 335–322 B.C.). Yet Aristotle describes what he understands to be the order of nature, of the household, among other things – namely what is right for man because man is man. But when Confucius said that "fathers should be fathers and sons should be sons," he was authoritatively describing the way that proper fathers and sons had always behaved. Enforcing such behavior and other aspects of how things were done was the whole purpose of law. The idea was that if law does not enforce doing things as they are, then things will cease to be as they are, and therefore as they should be. Reality's authority is also the reason why telling the truth about the world is essential. Until 1905, the deeply Confucian Chinese imperial civil service enforced that law.

In short, stability was the objective of traditional Chinese political theory. Just as fathers had to do certain things to maintain the family, so emperors had to fulfill their duty to maintain order. And if they didn't do the things that pertain to them, or did them badly, then things ceased to be as they were and should be, and the social fabric unraveled from the top. While "losing the mandate of heaven" remains a nebulous concept, clearly the thrust of the idea is that when rulers don't deliver stability, they bring obligations to an end.

Traditional Chinese despotism, then, was anything but revolutionary. Nor did it pit one part of society against another. It was not about class warfare or racial warfare, much less about revolution. Nor was it even oligarchical – an alliance of the powerful, entitled ones against the masses. It was about securing imperial power while interfering with the masses' orderly, predictable lives only to extract labor and obedience from them. China knew only the choice between stable despotism and chaos.

China, Communism & totalitarianism

Upper-middle-class students who had sojourned in London, Paris, and Berlin brought Communism to China in the early 1920s. Zhou Enlai was one of 1,200 of these. Academically trained, Zhou absorbed Marxism–Leninism and helped transition the then-nationalist Mao Tse-tung to it. There is no evidence that Mao (or anyone else in the Chinese Communist Party) understood or cared about Karl Marx's thought *qua* thought. Mao's *Little Red Book* (1964) is Marxist gobbledygook, but it does reflect Marxism's un-Chinese essence: tear down the pillars of the house and build anew.

Chinese Communists also adopted Lenin's construct of the Party as the ultimate weapon of conquest and power. From the 1920s to '40s, in China as everywhere else, would-be Communists were preoccupied with building cadres for the Party. Yet China, from the 1920s on, was in the throes of civil war. Mao and friends were building and wielding their own army for it, too. Thinking of those leaders as Party cadres in the Leninist sense seemed logical. Chinese history would also have led them to think of Party cells as eventual substitutes for the defunct imperial bureaucracy that had run the country for thousands of years.

But whereas stability had been the imperial bureaucracy's purpose, war was the Party's purpose – total war to abolish all that was old and replace it with something that no one could define but that required complete denial of the present. That, or perhaps Mao's insatiable hunger for power, negated all manner of law, thereby denouncing stability and Confucius himself. Thus did Mao dictate and superintend all manner of un-Chinese, untenable ventures, chiefly the superseding of the family with communes and the organization of economic activity into collectives. That chaos is what made Communist China a place of famine and fear. Unpredictability, not harshness, is what made Mao's rule unacceptable. We think of Mao's reign as totalitarian. For the Chinese, the term "revolution" is more meaningful and more frightening.

That very superintendence over a vast land and a billion people, however, made it inevitable that the Party cadre would take the place, and eventually adapt into the role, of the old imperial bureaucracy. Once Deng Xiaoping had defeated the last of the Maoists in 1978, these officials transmuted into their imperial predecessors – minus the competence. But that did not matter in the most important respect. Stability, allowing the rebirth of family and private economy, was enough to satisfy the modest demands of ordinary Chinese. The "mandate of heaven" does not seem to require more.

By the early 2000s, it really did not seem that anything happening in Chinese society might hurt America. The number of card-carrying Communists on American university faculties may still be higher than the number of serious Communists within China itself.

Far from making, never mind exporting, revolution, the Chinese Communist Party seemed satisfied that the people were eating better than ever and enjoying luxuries such as air conditioning. And although the Party cadres themselves rose and fell by the laws of favor, they administered a scrupulously fair and demanding system of academic exams by which ordinary people could make or break their futures. It seemed as if China had reverted to something like its millennial normality. In some ways, it had. Indeed, the quiet growth in China of a seemingly export-friendly version of something that we think of as totalitarianism was more important for us than for the Chinese.

Totalitarianism & social control

Let us see how a phenomenon that has developed in China over the past generation more fully than elsewhere, one that we Westerners call totalitarian, now threatens us.

"Totalitarian," to Westerners, describes a ruler's attempt to exert control over someone's rightful autonomy, regardless of the power grab's success, because we assume that we have rights that natural law forbids be taken from us. Property may be the most obvious of these. Your life, liberty, and pursuit of happiness are also naturally, inalienably your own. Mussolini first used the term "*totalitarismo*" in reference to his boast of "everything within the state, nothing outside the state, nothing against the state," even though his regime's aims were hardly as ambitious as the goals of those who have sought to remake humanity – such as the perpetrators of the French Revolution and those inspired by Marxism– Leninism. We Westerners believe that any uninvited attempt to control what is ours is inherently unlawful and illegitimate.

In China, however, law has coexisted very well with all manner and degree of despotism and social control. So long as there remains stability and regularity in people's lives, the waxing and waning of China's bedrock despotism has not affected its legitimacy. But unquestioning acceptance of despotism has made China a fertile petri dish for the growth of the latest virus: a computer-enforced "social-credit" system of societal control.

Always and everywhere, rulers seem to be in search of rationalizations and means of increasing their power over the ruled. They call upon religion or patriotism, invent or adopt pseudoscientific creeds, foster hopes, fears, and panics, and of course use any and all technological advances in service of their quest.

The unprecedented opportunity for social control offered by advances in computer technology, and the Chinese government's successful use of it for that purpose, combined with the Chinese people's matter-of-fact acquiescence, has led – misled, I believe – Western leaders to imagine that something like a "social-credit" system is transferable to the West.

THE SPECTER OF CHINESE CIVILIZATION

Few thoughtful people ever imagined that computer technology would be anything but a mortal peril for human liberty and a boon for the power-hungry. That is why, pretty much everywhere, enthusiasm for modern data-processing's promises of efficiency, personal connectivity, and the widespread flow of information were accompanied by at least some worry about how easily this tool could become the key to a totalitarianism more rigorous than had ever been imagined.

Everywhere, that is, except in China, because the Chinese people's historical and habitual acceptance of despotic authority obviates questions concerning the legitimacy of using "big data," or anything else, to serve government power. Such use involves the coordination of state and corporate activities to rate the actions and thoughts of individuals relative to authoritative priorities, then to reward and punish these individuals based on their behavior – by making certain ratings a condition for travel, for instance. Not incidentally, in China the use of computer-aided surveillance for enforcing laws and social norms has coincided with a decrease in its historically high level of social cohesion.

Social credit

Nothing could be more Chinese than lists containing criteria of personal behavior, and even of opinion – by which rulers may manage individuals by directing, judging, rewarding, and punishing them. But even in China there is no single integrated system for rating financial, political, or moral behavior, in part because the standards being enforced vary from place to place, and with the changing concerns of officials.

Regardless of the above, the very existence of the databases, their acceptance, and the fact that they may be used for all manner of enforcement have enabled Chinese officials to bring the full weight of government and society to bear on any matters important to them. Using data management to cut and shape the flow of information, mobilizing support with rewards while punishing dissent, has made today's Chinese leadership more unchallengeable than the emperors of old ever were.

Keep foremost in mind that these new tools only confirm Chinese rule's main, distinctive, despotic characteristic: in China, ruling does not involve the least bit of persuasion. The ruler does not convince the ruled of anything, and he does not try. The ruler rules exclusively by command and coercion. No wonder Westerners, who must convince the ruled to agree, or suffer dissent, envy the Chinese and yearn to imitate them.

But Westerners fascinated with social credit in China neglect the radical difference between what it means there and what it would mean here. The lingering presence of the Confucian tradition suggests that the criteria for rating people must have much to do with how things have been done and continue to be done, and that any system must be administered in a stable, sustainable manner. The stricter the demands, the less tolerant of change. Our looming Western tyranny is quite the opposite. Not only for logistical reasons is it impossible to imagine a Chinese social-credit system forcing people to deny the difference between men and women, or even to utter the words "father, mother, son, daughter." Besides, China's regime has no interest in such things, unlike the gender-obsessed commissars found throughout Western governments and academia.

The Specter of Chinese Civilization

Information management & the model

Indeed, it seems that contemporary Western regimes, ours in America especially, are interested in little else besides frivolous questions of identity and how such questions may be used to control the population. Western businessmen, political leaders, and government bureaucrats have always looked enviously at the Chinese population's docility. Willful and ignorant, the Western elites see China with their own agendas foremost in mind and see no reason why something that works in China should not work in America – especially if they, the allegedly enlightened elite, want it to.

In fairness, we must note that China's complex foreignness lends itself to misinterpretation. The original Western Sinologist, Matteo Ricci (1552–1610), came to understand China's Confucian subtleties only after a lifetime of study. Today's Chinese government has overlain those principles with pure will, right down to the words themselves. The radical simplification of contemporary Chinese orthography has made it almost impossible even for Chinese to read Confucius in the original.

Still, the main reason why Western leaders misunderstand China is that they have never learned or appreciated their own civilization. Our overlords ask: Why is it that Westerners, Americans above all, won't simply do what they are told? Why do we insist on coming to our own conclusions about right and wrong, better and worse? Why do we noisily demand informed consent?

What contemporary Western leaders miss is what the Book of Genesis revealed, and Greek philosophy clarified: that the world is made according to, in the words of the Declaration of

Independence, the "laws of Nature and of Nature's God," and that all humans are equally creatures of the same God, equally subject to those laws; that understanding and living by these laws is every human being's equal right and duty; and hence that, rightly to rule one another, we humans must convince one another. In other words: acting properly depends neither on tradition nor on power, but on right and wrong, better and worse, objectively true.

Although even the wokest of the corporate leaders and government officials who run America do not openly deny this foundational civilizational pillar, and thereby affirm the duty of ordinary people to obey rulers blindly, the emergence of the technical means by which to restrict and manage the information available to the general population has spurred many among them to try working around that pillar. They seek to obviate informed consent, by more or less forcefully managing the flow of information.

For many of our rulers, this does not pose problems of principle because, having thoughtlessly internalized the notion that truth and error, right and wrong, are relative (or as Marxists put it, "superstructural") to the realities of interest, they effectively believe that power makes its own right. In practice, they agree with Plato's Thrasymachus, who maintained that right is everywhere the interest of the stronger, and with China's rulers as well.

Networked computers make it possible to spread favored versions of events – "our truth," rather than *the* truth – and to discourage, if not punish, the circulation of disfavored versions of events, which nothing prevents us from calling "inaccurate," "problematic," or "disinformational." Those who control our information are careful not to label material that they thus stigmatize as "false," lest someone defend it as factually true. Reference to objective reality is dangerous, and it is far better to stick to trials of power.

Consider just one example of the elite ability to control the flow of information under the guise of protecting the population. Speaking about efforts to discredit, restrict, and shut out of circulation non-favored ideas about the COVID-19 epidemic, the Surgeon General of the United States said, "we expect more from our technology companies.... We're asking them to monitor misinformation ... to consistently take action against misinformation super-spreaders on their platforms." The then–White House press secretary, Jen Psaki, seconded that: the Biden administration had, she said, "increased disinformation research and tracking." It was "flagging problematic posts for Facebook that spread disinformation." She did not quite say that it was "ordering" Facebook to act upon its judgment about what is information and what is disinformation and what the difference might be. But she added, "We're working with doctors and medical professionals ... to connect medical experts ... who are popular with their audiences with ... accurate information and boost trusted content. So we're helping get trusted content out there."

In short, the current presidential administration wants companies such as Facebook to do more censoring of thoughts that do not fit its agenda than those companies are already doing. The force of that censorship comes mostly from the consensus that exists within the ruling class that thoughts that do not flow from itself, that do not reflect its agendas, should be effectively banished so that the public will know only "trusted content." But trusted by whom? Computers do not create the ruling class's unanimity of interest and hence of opinion. They are neither more nor less than a means of imposing that unanimity on a general population whose recalcitrance the rulers must fear.

They must fear it because, although the substance of what they demand is often not as harsh as what Chinese rulers demand of their subjects, Americans are not civilizationally conditioned to accept demands as part of the world's natural order, as Chinese subjects are. Take the imposition of internal passports as a condition of employment, travel, and so on. The Chinese do not need to cite public health or any other excuse to enforce such a stricture. But no excuse may convince many Americans to accept them, especially since those who tout them do so on a transparently partisan basis. But our oligarchs bolster and impose their demands with such force and reach as to create what might appear to be a new model of civilization, one dangerously ignorant of the traditions that have allowed Western civilization, and America especially, to flourish throughout history.

Revolutionary civilization is impossible

In the twenty-first century, an oligarchy has replaced the American republic. The people's elected representatives had previously ruled by persuading each other and their voters. But the distinction between public office and private power has given way to the criterion of proximity to a community of powerful individuals and institutions. In a republic, power derives its legitimacy from the voters. In oligarchies like our current model, power is exercised by persons who control the country's institutions. They don't think of themselves as citizens, but as "stakeholders." Their legitimacy derives from each other's support. How did stakeholders replace citizens? Who are these stakeholders, and by what right do they rule?

As government grew in size and power, it drew unto itself the practical allegiance of the country's most powerful private persons. Even without formal legal provisions such as that of Italy's 1926 National Council of Corporations (Italian fascism's defining feature) or the U.S. National Industrial Recovery Act of 1933 (partially invalidated by the courts), prolonged association between regulators and regulated, between administrators and administered, soon erased distinctions between them. Seamlessly, the same people changed from one role to the other. Not being wholly responsible to government or to private business, they ended up as the effective owners of the "stakes" they have in the system.

Agreements within "public–private partnerships" also differ in nature from ones made among elected representatives. The latter, as James Madison argued, draw out the "deliberate sense" of the people by adjusting their interests politically. But regulatory decisions, indeed administrative decisions by their very nature, are made on the real or pretend basis of expertise. But who judges expertise, if not the ones who pretend to have it? And if these experts also dispense the money that gives access to credentials, then there occurs the situation about which President Dwight Eisenhower warned us: "public policy could itself become the captive of a scientific-technological elite" because a "government contract becomes virtually a substitute for intellectual curiosity."

And as Ike warned, the process did proceed through the "power of money" via federal "project allocations." Beginning in the 1960s, Congress lavishly funded multiple mandates to rid America of poverty, ignorance, racial discrimination, and much more. Each of these in turn mandated a bureaucracy to dispense the money. These in turn created classes of people who lived by these moneys and, along with the bureaucrats, took ownership, thereby becoming stakeholders of the programs.

Oligarchy is the replacement of representative government by the melding of public and private power with the administrative state. Throughout history, most oligarchies have united around the stakeholders' primary common interest in orderly rent-seeking. Typically, oligarchies have nothing to do with ideas of right and wrong, never mind with ideology. And if they form out of a political party, that party is all about oligarchy itself.

But ours is not a typical oligarchy. The sense of superiority to the rest of America had been the animating force behind the Progressive movement around the turn of the twentieth century. From their embryo, the disparate parts of the American administrative state/oligarchy shared this sense. Beginning in the 1960s, however, the will to hurt and to demean the rest of the population grew among these stakeholders, to the point that today, this vengeful approach overshadows and endangers their very power.

This happened because the tasks that these public/private institutions were empowered to fulfill always had something hostile, vindictive about them. Rid America of poverty? Can we do that without blaming our least favorite people for its existence? What about ridding America of racial discrimination? Clearly, our least favorite people are responsible for it and must be made more than a little uncomfortable. And if that takes raising the level of racial animus, it's for a good cause. As the power of stakeholders grew, other kinds of modern progressives lent support and demanded coequal attention to their grievances against the rest of the American people. That is why America's ruling oligarchy is a coalition based on little but grievances, which the several sets of stakeholders usually do not even share. These are bitter, often screaming, grievances, many of which have long since morphed into sheer hate. The oligarchy's opponents are, in the telling of American elites, responsible for everything from the black murder rate to the frying of the planet.

America's oligarchy is made up of diverse elements that have little in common other than an indifference to or loathing of Western civilization in general and of the American republic in particular. Since members of the oligarchy support each other's claims – over which they have no control – by the iron law of political necessity, there is no logical end to those claims. That is yet another reason why our oligarchy's modus operandi relies so heavily on cutting off at the source any and all circulation of facts and arguments that would cause any set of stakeholders publicly to argue its case – an argument they might lose and that would surely upset other members of the coalition. This is why Google's and Facebook's censorship is essential to the oligarchy's continued power.

Our oligarchy no longer even pretends that the commands it issues about what may or may not be discussed, what is "trustworthy" versus "misleading," derive from anything other than what its members – very much including the government – demand here and now.

Forcefully restricting and managing the information available to the general population empowers and institutionalizes the division between rulers and ruled, and does so in a partisan, even tribal way. In America this practice is revolutionary because it so explicitly destroys the theory and practice of equality that had been the American republic's defining characteristic, and because it does so on behalf of a part of the population. Google, Facebook, and Twitter, among many others, not only restrict what disfavored people may tell each other. They also limit certain segments of the population's ability to learn from history and the great store of Western knowledge. They have arrogated to themselves the power to decide who is allowed to appear on the national stage by retaining the ability to wipe out whole accounts, as if their holders never existed. Moreover, they prevent the disfavored ones from using their platforms to complain. They do all this on behalf of the bureaucratic elite that runs most government in America, and whose officials adjudicate disputes.

Clearly the American oligarchy manages information differently, and for a radically different purpose, from China's tyrannical state. Whereas Chinese rulers demand and get obedience on behalf of a millennialist mono-ethnic (or at least they so pretend), nonpartisan country (the title Communist having lost practical significance), America's rulers demand it on behalf of allegedly aggrieved persons who never cease to stress their own difference from the ruled. The truly powerless Americans are, rather than objects of compassion, merely contemptuous in the eyes of the elite. That same contempt applies to the country as a whole and the Western civilization that has nourished it. Because the substance of the oligarchy's demands changes at will and convenience, compromising with them is impossible. So· is obtaining peace by surrender. One may search history without finding examples of tribal rule-by-aggravation lasting very long.

After the crisis, what?

Ever-intensifying tribal identity, tribal hostility, and tribal warfare usually result in war. But whether by civil war, or by some sort of reformist Thermidorean, Napoleonic, or Khruschevian regime – or goodness knows what – our collective madness will someday end. This by no means counsels complacency towards how this madness may affect the kinds of lives of which Americans may be capable in the future.

What is now America's ruling culture has been gestating and marking Americans for more than a half century. The effects are all too obvious, and in some senses are worse than what the Soviets inflicted on the Russian people. Our society's tone-setters have devalued marriage, and families now raise children in a way that is arguably more violent than the Soviets did in their most virulent phase. The Soviets never descended to devaluing academic excellence, especially in math and science.

Sure as we may be that the woke regime will eventually collapse, we can be just as sure that it will leave behind millions of people who share its culture, unable and unwilling to live in one they regard as alien. We cannot know how many Americans have joined that culture. Even their very presence among us will tend to suck, pull, push, and prod the rest of us into a lifestyle far nastier than anything in ancient or even modern China.

Who will oppose them, and with what culture? Many on the right, justifiably fearful of their vanishing way of life, have chosen to defend it by defending freedom itself, abstractly. But freedom is valuable only in relation to the good. Noble as it may be to defend the right to lie, that right is worth defending only if it is part of a civilization that values truth. Nobody lives or dies for freedom abstractly.

The American republic's Founders did not do that, and neither should today's Republicans try to do it. The Founders articulated specific grievances of which they wished to rid themselves. And they chose to live by "the laws of Nature and of Nature's God." These laws were no more abstractions than were the grievances. Nor was their love for those laws abstract. These people did not carry their Bibles as any sort of cultural badge. They read them to keep in mind what was expected of them and of one another.

Our ruling oligarchy has made it socially difficult even to think about the difference between what is right and wrong. This itself presents us with an important crossroads. Eliminating the intellectual and moral conversation that made the American republic unique has been the oligarchs' effect if not also their objective. Their success in this enterprise haunts America's future. China does not.

Editors' note: Angelo M. Codevilla, who died on September 21, 2021, was reviewing final edits on this chapter at the time of his death.

Unprecedented

MICHAEL ANTON

THE THEME OF THIS BOOK is "Western civilization at the crossroads." Far be it from me to doubt that the West is on the precipice of something enormous. But "crossroads" implies a map. Do we have one? Is a piece of paper showing the way forward – whether predictive or hopeful – even possible?

I've noticed that a lot of people more or less "on my side," or who see things basically as I do, are extremely confident that they know what is going to happen next. Their certainty is entirely independent of what they think they know.

Some believe that the end – the collapse of present ruling arrangements – is imminent, if not tomorrow or next week, then soon, within a year or five. Others assert that the present regime is stable and not only can but will last for decades or even centuries. Some insist that the regime will fall of its own incompetence, others that its end will require an external push – which some are certain will come, and others are equally sure will not.

When I have thought about this, I have been in some part inclined to the opinion that present arrangements are unstable and may be approaching their end. Yet in thinking it through further, I am forced to admit that our times are marked by so many unprecedented trends and events that making predictions seems foolhardy.

But before going into those differences, let's first consider the one historical parallel that all sides of this debate draw on for precedent: the rise, peak, decline, and fall of Rome. At first glance, the two cases seem to have a lot in common. Not only was the United States founded by men educated in the classics who took Roman pseudonyms and named the government's top legislative body after Rome's, and not only did those founders revive republicanism after centuries of abeyance following the transformation of the Roman Republic into an empire, but our country's history itself seems to have tracked Rome's, if not precisely then certainly thematically.

Both Rome and America were founded by kings – or, in our case, under the auspices of a king. In both instances, the descendants of those kings ruled in ways their subjects found intolerable and were overthrown. Both peoples then established a mixed-republican form of government, with monarchical, aristocratic, and popular elements. Both of those governments were, at first, weighted toward their aristocratic elements but gradually – owing in part to popular discontent and strife – became more balanced and eventually biased toward the popular element. Both societies fought constant wars, self-justified as "defensive" but more often than not expansionist. Both rapidly conquered what we might call their immediate "neighborhoods" – the Italian peninsula and major Mediterranean islands, the North American continent, respectively – and then went on to win major wars against competing "superpowers," in the process becoming world-bestriding hegemons. Indeed, we may say that no other power in history, save for perhaps the British Empire, acquired such extensive spheres of influence and so dominated their respective eras for so long. If other empires held more territory, or perhaps technically lasted longer, none exerted nearly as much enduring influence on the rest of the world.

The Roman case

In Rome's case, its government formally made the transition from republic to empire after a long expansion that bloated the treasury, increased the size and power of the military, concentrated wealth in the hands of a few who controlled not just the economy but the government, and impoverished ordinary citizens. While much of that may sound familiar, much is different, making the analogy (like all such historical comparisons) inexact. Rome conquered and directly administered territory throughout the entire Mediterranean basin and over most of the (then-) known world. America's "empire," by contrast, is quasi-metaphoric or at the very least indirect; the only external territories of any consequence it controls are Puerto Rico and Guam. Then there are all the differences in religion, philosophy, society, economics, technology, and so on, far too numerous to list. (One might also ask: where's *our* bloated treasury?)

America has yet formally to transform (if it ever will) from republic to empire. Yet in all important respects, our country is no longer a republic, much less a democracy, but rather a kind of hybrid corporate-administrative oligarchy. This lack of formal transition causes some to speculate that America is in the "late republican" stage, with the republic (it is alleged, or hoped) soon to fall to a "Caesar." Those who assert that the transition, however informal its appearance, has already happened are more likely to place America in the "late imperial" stage, i.e., much closer to total collapse and replacement by an entirely new order.

All such speculations presuppose the truth of the classical theory known as the "cycle of regimes." Just as Rome was born, grew, matured, peaked, declined, and eventually fell, so will – and must – America. Cycle theory predicts that every more or less good regime – whether monarchy, aristocracy, or democracy – falls when it inevitably becomes overbearing and odious. Thus do monarchies degenerate into tyrannies, which are replaced by aristocracies that decay into oligarchies, which are overthrown by democracies that descend into mob-rule or even anarchy. In that case, we should expect our present oligarchy, sooner or later, to give way to democracy.

While that possibility cannot be dismissed out of hand, the prospect seems laughable. If there is to be, as cycle theory predicts, a popular revolt against our corrupt oligarchy, it would seem much more likely to be led by a charismatic, centralizing figure who ascends to the leadership of the popular party and then installs himself as the head of government – in other words, Caesarism. And even that would depend on a Caesar of sufficient talent and institutional support, as well as a sufficient level of spirit and virtue in the people (and on much else besides).

More fundamentally, classic cycle theory presupposes an ethnically, linguistically, and religiously unified people. Indeed, in his *Politics*, Aristotle says that "dissimilarity of stock is conducive to factional conflict," i.e., ethnic differences in and of themselves, irrespective of disagreements over regime form (typically few versus many), can drive revolution. Aristotle seems to admit the possibility of assimilation: dissimilarity, he says, leads to conflict "until a cooperative spirit develops." But he cites no examples, forcing one to wonder how likely it is for this theoretical possibility to be actualized in the real world. It seems, instead, that the fundamental conflict between the few and the many emerges only where the more fundamental conflict between differing peoples is absent. Where it is not, the few and the many alike rally to their fellow ethnics; ethnicity itself, rather than "class," is their prime motivator.

Multi-ethnic polities are hardly unknown to history. Of these, Aristotle gives several examples – all of which ended up fighting civil wars along ethnic lines.

The most common (one may say only) way that multi-ethnic societies have been successfully governed is centrally, from the top, by some form of one-man rule, whether monarchical, Caesarist, or tyrannical. This, ultimately, is how Rome "solved" the problem of admitting so many foreigners to citizenship, to say nothing of its far-flung conquest of peoples whom it never made citizens. In more recent times, one may think of the Austro-Hungarian Empire and Tito's Yugoslavia.

America today

Consider, now, the contemporary United States of America. At first glance, it seems to belie Aristotle's implied assertion that regime-ending ethnic conflict is unavoidable wherever more than one group lives under the same government. Americans pride themselves, and their country, on their exceptional track record of assimilating peoples from all over the world.

Yet before we congratulate ourselves overmuch, let us reflect, first, on the fact that the United States has not merely abandoned but utterly repudiated the traditional understanding of assimilation, which is now denounced by all elite opinion as "racist" and evil. Not only does no American institution encourage (much less demand) assimilation, they all foment the opposite. Immigrants to America are exhorted to embrace their native cultures and taught that the country to which they've chosen to immigrate is the worst in world history, whose people and institutions are intent on harming them, and that their own cultures are infinitely superior. In this respect, one supposes, immigrants *are* encouraged to "assimilate" – to the anti-Americanism of the average Oberlin professor.

Be that as it may, no nation in recorded history has ever willingly opened its doors to millions of immigrants only to insist that they must never adapt to the traditional ways of their new country – indeed, insisting that they forever remain as foreign as the day they arrived. Similarly, no country in recorded history has ever welcomed millions with the message that their new country, along with its existing citizens, are inherently evil and out to get them.

Second, assimilation works best among peoples with some common underlying similarity, whether political, linguistic, ethnic, religious, or cultural (preferably a combination of all these). Its effectiveness declines as the differences among the disparate peoples increase. Historically, the closer in the above categories an immigrant group was to founding-stock Americans, the more quickly and smoothly its members assimilated. American immigration policy and practice has drifted steadily away from prioritizing this practice. In particular, since the passage of the 1965 Immigration Act and the de facto (since the 1970s at least) nonenforcement of America's borders and immigration laws, newcomers to America have become more and more distant – not just from existing Americans but from one another. America now takes in, and has been importing for more than fifty years, people from every part of the globe, of every faith, speaking every language. This, too, has never before happened in world history.

Third is the size of the wave. Precise numbers are hard to come by, but if we count immigrants legal and illegal plus all their direct descendants, then something like a hundred million newcomers have arrived in America since 1965. Only fourteen countries today have total populations exceeding that figure. In 1965, there were just under two hundred million Americans. Today it is estimated that 333 million live within our borders. At least two-thirds of that growth has been immigrant-driven. This large a migration wave, in so short a time, to one country, from so many different sources, has also never happened before in human history. Need a "respectable" source to vouch for that? Here's Bill Clinton in 1998:

> But now we are being tested again – by a new wave of immigration larger than any in a century, far more diverse than any in our history. Each year, nearly a million people come legally to America. Today, nearly one in ten people in America was born in another country; one in five schoolchildren are from immigrant families. Today, largely because of immigration, there is no majority race in Hawaii or Houston or New York City. Within five years there will be no majority race in our largest state, California. In a little more than fifty years, there will be no majority race in the United States [applause]. No other nation in history has gone through demographic change of this magnitude in so short a time.

Note the applause. The venue of the above speech was a university commencement: a sitting president addressing freshly minted college graduates and their parents, i.e., the elite speaking to the elite. Demographic decline was literally applauded. And this is only one example. Mere months ago, when the Census announced that, for the first time in American history, the white population had declined in absolute numbers, *The Tonight Show*'s audience cheered. No native-born population of any country has ever literally cheered its own dispossession.

That which cannot be said

The "Great Replacement" is happening, not just in America but throughout the West. Elites both deny and affirm it. When they write op-eds in *The New York Times* entitled "We Can Replace Them," that's a good thing and the phenomenon under discussion is absolutely right and just. When you notice and express the mildest wish not to be replaced, it's a racist conspiracy theory that you are evil for even mentioning – your evil being further proof that you deserve to be replaced. They get to say it; you're required not merely to pretend that you didn't hear it but also to insist that they never said it. No majority stock in any nation has ever deliberately sought its own replacement, much less insisted that those who might have misgivings lie to themselves that it's not happening.

The "Great Replacement" is not just happening; under the Biden-Harris regime, it is accelerating. Among the few promises Biden has kept are those not to build a single new inch of the border wall or to enforce immigration laws. As a result, illegal migrants are pouring across the southern border at an unprecedented rate. The ridiculous former practice of "catch-and-release" – catch an illegal immigrant, release him on American soil – has been replaced by "catch-and-bus" or even "catch-and-airlift." The U.S.

government places illegal border-crossers on buses and planes and distributes them throughout the heartland, unannounced, often followed by official denials. Naturally, none of these people is vetted in any way – not for COVID, which had the rest of us in semi-permanent lockdown, nor for criminal records or anything else. Couple this with the regime's policy to settle throughout middle America as many unvetted Afghans as possible – some of whom are likely terrorists, several of whom have already committed sex crimes – and it is fair to describe current practice as demographic warfare. The concept is not exactly new; tyrants have been known from time immemorial to move populations around so as to hold conquests more securely. What's unprecedented is a regime importing foreigners to harm its own people.

The question of immigration is inseparable from that of race. "Critical Race Theory," much in the news lately, is but the latest iteration of intellectual and academic anti-whiteness that has been central to leftist ideology since the mid-1960s. The ur-specimen is Susan Sontag's 1967 belch that "the white race is the cancer of human history." Examples are so numerous today that cataloguing them all would be a full-time job for an entire think tank – but a pointless one, since the Left will in the same breath deny and affirm their own words quoted back to them: "We didn't say that, and it's good that we did." Many whites, apparently, believe they *deserve* to be replaced because their race makes them uniquely, and irredeemably, evil. While cultural self-loathing is hardly unknown to history, I know of none so explicitly race-based or widespread – or so eager to pursue self-abnegation all the way to the end.

This hatred of the core stock of the nation, by other members of that same stock, also appears to be unprecedented. Examples can be found of a new elite rising to preeminence above an older one, which it then displaces with prejudice. But of a ruling class coming to despise its own (broadly speaking) ethnic group and seeking ways to rob their fellow co-ethnics of power, standing, and influence? I can't think of any other such cases.

The matter becomes even more complicated when one reflects that this is mostly an intra-white civil war. One group of whites pronounces the entire white race evil, seeks policies to hurt it, but somehow exempts itself. So far, these upper-caste whites have found ways to protect their own privilege but haven't developed consistent rhetoric to defend that privilege. They appear to believe that no matter how much anti-white poison they vomit or how many destructive policies they enact, none will ever blow back on them. In particular, they seem to believe that the "allies" in whom they stir up anti-white hatred will never turn and bite them; at least, they appear not to have seriously considered the possibility. This situation, too, is unprecedented.

Tyranny old & new

Tyrants or ruling classes that despoil their countries for personal gain are nothing new. If that were all we had today, our situation would be much more understandable. And we do, in part, have that. Our ruling class is rich and rapacious – rich *because* rapacious, and eager to be richer still by taking what little you have left.

Yet elite enthusiasms extend well beyond mere greed. There is a malice in them atypical to the native despot, one found historically only or largely among the most punitive conquerors. A tyrant fears a healthy population, to be sure, because such is always a threat to his power. This fear typically inspires little beyond efforts to ensure that the population is dependent and unarmed – two aims of our overlords, it need hardly be added.

But our elites also go much further. They seem determined to make the American population fat, weak, ugly, lethargic, drug-addled, screen-addicted, and hyper-sexualized, the men effeminate and the women masculine. Those last two actually barely scratch the surface of the agenda, which includes turning males into "females" and vice versa – or into any one of a potentially infinite number of "genders." (The number varies depending on which source you check; sixty-three is the highest I could find. Needless to say, no establishment source stops at "two.")

The regime promotes every imaginable historic form of degeneracy – and then invents new ones undreamt of by Caligula, the Borgias, or Catherine the Great. All these it pushes through every available media channel, social and legacy, in programming and advertising alike, even in books stocked in elementary-school libraries. As I write, the Virginia governor's race is being roiled by the presence in said libraries of *Gender Queer: A Memoir*, an illustrated "children's" book as sexually explicit as 1970s hard-core pornography – and arguably illegal to boot, since it depicts minors. One candidate for governor and his supporters indignantly insisted that this kind of material *must* be forced on your kids at public expense and that only Nazis object. Degeneracy in tyrants is of course as old as the hills, but prior despots had the "decency," if one could call it that, to restrict their perversions to the satisfaction of their own private pleasures. To force degeneracy on the whole of society, with the explicit intent of bringing the rest us to our knees, literally and figuratively – that, I think, has never happened before.

An odd feature of our time is the coupling of mass hyper-sexualization with mass barrenness. Some argue, plausibly, that the link is direct: hyper-sexualization disconnected from procreation inevitably leads to fewer babies. The degree to which crashing fertility is simply an effect of modernity versus a deliberate plan by our rulers is an open question. It is certainly true that every economically and technologically developed society, regardless of region, culture, race, or religion, suffers from cratering birthrates.

But it's also true that our rulers advocate and celebrate careerism, consumerism, self-centeredness, casual sex, delayed marriage, (let us say) "non-fecund" couplings, and, where and if all that fails, small families – "for the environment," you understand. In other words, when and where the (allegedly) inexorable process of modernity is overcome by the innate human desire for love and family, the regime eagerly steps in with propaganda to bully men and women out of such longings. I suppose there is a near-historical precedent for this, namely China's one-child policy, in effect from 1980 to 2015. But that was implemented to relieve (it was thought) a looming Malthusian crisis, a fear that cannot reasonably apply to contemporary America, whose birthrate is 1.64 and falling like a stone. China itself, whose leaders want its people to live on, abandoned the policy. Meanwhile, America unofficially does everything it can to suppress native births. Has this ever happened before in a country not even plausibly facing a "population crisis"?

The promotion of ugliness deserves special attention. The autocrats of old wanted to be known for their patronage of beauty, the arts, and great works. This is one meaning of Shelley's "Ozymandias," and also of Augustus's boast that he found Rome a city of brick and left it a city of marble (to say nothing of having commissioned the *Aeneid*). A stroll through any city in

Europe, and in most of the Americas, finds the same sentiment everywhere – until about the middle of the twentieth century, when suddenly everything turned brutalist, and brutally ugly, and not just the buildings, but the art, the literature, the music, almost everything.

One attempts to state the following as delicately as possible, even though regime propaganda on this score is anything but delicate, but today the ugliness extends to people. One hesitates also to say anything that could be interpreted as praise of underwear ads, but, within living memory, the sirens of Times Square billboards were lithe and lovely; today they are, quite deliberately, obese and angry. That is, when they're not cross-dressers or pierced like an East Village junkie and tattooed like a C-list porn star. All this, we are commanded to believe, is "beautiful," though no healthy person does. The point seems to be humiliation: forcing us little people to say "the thing which is not." That trick is also as old as the hills, but the deliberate promotion of ugliness seems to be a new way to play it. Antiquity abounded in wicked tyrants, yet try to find an ancient statue anywhere near as hideous as a modern lingerie model.

But in terms of what we choose to elevate, nothing illustrates the perversity of present America more than the deification of George Floyd. There are now monuments to him all over the country that are treated as sacred. In a rare instance when one is defaced, the resultant outcry resembles the Athenian people's reaction to the desecration of the Hermai. One may insist that George Floyd did not deserve to die the way he did and still see that neither did he live his life so as to make the possibility remote. He was convicted of eight crimes and charged with or detained for at least nineteen (though one must here concede the difficulty of finding reliable relevant information, since unflattering facts about Floyd's life are effectively suppressed and are taboo to discuss). The worst of his crimes was an armed robbery in which he pointed a gun at the belly of a woman who may (or may not) have been pregnant. Floyd's admirers insist she wasn't, but more careful sources assert only that no one has ever definitively proved she was. Floyd was the father of five children, from whose lives he was by all accounts absent, and none of whose mothers he ever married. At the time of his death, Floyd was in the process of being arrested for yet another crime and was not cooperating with the arresting officers. A serial drug abuser, he had in his system not just methamphetamine but a potentially lethal dose of fentanyl – an extremely dangerous synthetic opioid – which may well have contributed to his death. Even if one fully accepts the trial court's finding that the drugs played no role, one must still admit that had Floyd only gotten into the back of the police vehicle as officers instructed, he could not have died in the way prosecutors (and the media) alleged. Above all, we must confront the painful fact that Floyd did not, according to moral standards that for centuries were taken for granted, live a life worthy of admiration, much less of veneration. Yet our society treats him as a saint, if not something higher. The pagan gods were not always well-behaved, to say the least. But has any people ever chosen such an undeserving object of worship?

Bad education

We may tie these points together under the broad rubric of "education," though that word is risibly inapt to what is "taught" today. The word's root is Latin and means "to lead forth" – that is, to coax out of imperfect but improvable human nature that which makes each human being better. Or, as the classics understood it, not merely to impart knowledge but also to form character.

In both respects, our system does the opposite. It teaches lies, attacks and suppresses truth, and encourages people to behave worse. It tells children to hate themselves (or their classmates) because of their race and to hate their country. It encourages boys to declare themselves girls, and vice versa. It badgers kids into professing themselves attracted to members of the same sex, or of all sixty-three sexes, regardless of, or despite, their natural inclination. It firehoses them with sexualized messaging and imagery, always taking care to decouple orgasmic self-indulgence from love and family.

The people who run the system, or many of them, can only be described as sadists. How sick does one's mind have to be to think it a good idea to teach a black kindergartner (through the taxpayer-financed public education system, no less) to hate his white classmates, or those white classmates to hate themselves? A sane society would call this child abuse.

The system now protects predators at the expense of the vulnerable and attacks parents who object. In Virginia, a boy in a skirt entered a girls' bathroom and raped a student. The school and the district hushed it up and transferred him to another school – where he did it again. When one victim's father complained at a school-board meeting, cops roughed him up and arrested him. The superintendent, principal, and all others in authority furiously denied that any assault had ever taken place – that is, except for the father's impassioned plea, which the school board referred to the Attorney General of the United States, who then ordered the FBI and U.S. attorneys to investigate outspoken parents as "domestic terrorists." This is not merely insane but deliberately evil. The Carthaginians cast living children into furnaces to satiate their (false) god Baal; we sacrifice our children's mental heath and adult futures to appease our false god Woki. *Plus ça change?*

(We may note in passing that when similar atrocities occurred in the pre-woke Catholic Church, an institution the ruling class feared and despised, demands for "accountability" were deafening. Today, the only sounds one hears are from establishmentarians and their Conservatism, Inc., enablers: this isn't happening, it's a "culture-war trope" ginned up by MAGA "racists," and anyway it's no big deal so lighten up.)

The most prevalent failures of education in history, it is widely accepted, have stemmed from a lack of it: failing to teach the poor basic skills such as reading and writing, or even deliberately depriving them of such learning. Now we have come full circle, but worse. We barely teach kids to read, write, or add anymore – indeed, the most "progressive" corners of the education system denounce such emphasis on standards and core knowledge as "white-supremacist." There's ample historical precedent for widespread illiteracy. But for teaching one's own citizens self-hatred, degeneracy, and despondency – without teaching them to read and write?

Barbarians at the gates

The typical tyrant enjoys wealth and power, which are easier to extract from a productive populace than from zombies. He therefore, typically, does not prioritize degrading his population beyond measures necessary to produce obedience. The serial humiliations inflicted on our people by its ruling class – not all of which, to say the least, generate profits – appear to be another element of contemporary life without historical precedent.

Crime is a case in point. No society, whether free or despotic, benefits from crime, all else being equal – though it's certainly true that a tyrant can find it useful to exempt his own partisans from criminal enforcement, and even to encourage them to terrorize his enemies. Criminals being criminals, this is a hard dynamic to keep from spinning out of control. In 2020, for instance, the ruling class unleashed BLM hordes and Antifa predators, plus assorted rioters and looters, to despoil and burn some 220 American cities.

Sacking was not uncommon in the ancient world. Rome was sacked many times, but always by foreigners and never at the instigation of her leading citizens: the senate never riled up the plebs to scorch the Capitoline. Yet in the summer of 2020, our ruling class actively encouraged, through state-aligned media, the repeated sacking of Manhattan, the very beating heart of the Davos Archipelago, where our richest and most powerful overlords live and work. They fired up mobs to trash huge swaths of Washington, D.C., their cherished imperial capital, which to this day has yet to recover. Why did they do that? Was there some nefarious plan to derive benefit that I don't understand? Or was this an instance of losing control of the shock troops? Either way, the events were unprecedented.

Then there are the related issues of technology and our fake economy. These subjects are far too large to explore here and so must be treated cursorily. Let us merely say that modern digital technology is unlike any previous "advance" in human history. It threatens not only to become man's master and destroyer (other technologies have also threatened that) but also to remake his very soul – or kill it.

The modern economy that technology enables is similarly anti-human. It deprives billions of the dignity of meaningful work at fair remuneration while it enriches a tiny minority adept at manipulating bits and bytes to no discernible purpose or benefit. The world has had to endure oligarchs for millennia. But our empty plutocrats create nothing but new ways to waste time and enervate the spirit. They are, like the technologies that make them rich and powerful, an entirely new phenomenon.

Finally, there is the endless insistence that every new dawn must begin a fresh Year Zero; we must start continually anew. What was acceptable yesterday is anathema today and will be more so tomorrow. All that came before must be swept aside and destroyed with extreme prejudice, on a rolling basis.

The most ferocious revolutionaries of yesteryear didn't do this. The Jacobins changed the calendar and guillotined a lot of nobles but otherwise allowed France to remain French. The Bolsheviks did not touch the Russian literary or concert canons; to the contrary, they celebrated both. Mao made an attempt to start over – until the more sensible Party bosses realized that the old man (and especially his wife) had lost their minds and were destroying China, sidelined him, and quietly put an end to the Cultural Revolution four years before formally declaring mission accomplished. The Ayatollah did not ban Nowruz or other cornerstones of Persian tradition beloved by the Iranian people, but which predated his puritanical version of Islam.

Our overlords, by contrast, insist on changing everything and will not stop until everything familiar is gone. When this is pointed out, they smirk about the "slippery-slope fallacy" and gleefully lie.

UNPRECEDENTED

That will never happen, they say, until they insist on it, and, once accomplished, move on to the next target. They are cultural locusts devouring everything in their path. If the internal "logic" (if one may use that word in this context) of their passionate hatred is allowed to play out, no statue can be left standing, no traditional holiday observed, no name unchanged. If that outcome does not come to pass, it will not be because those driving toward it have a change of heart, nor is it likely to be because the Right suddenly becomes effective in opposition. It will rather be because the locusts destroy too many of the country's remaining functioning parts too soon, causing the system to collapse before their program is complete, thereby making further "progress" impossible.

Any one of the above elements would appear to be unprecedented; just a few of them in combination surely are. All of them together?

How, therefore, can anyone be confident that he "knows" what is going to happen – whether imminent collapse, drawn-out decline, or centuries of tyranny?

The end?

If forced to bet, I would have to place my chips somewhere between imminent collapse and drawn-out decline. I occasionally read theories of triple bank-shots and four-dimensional chess – they really know what they're doing! – only to marvel. Our regime cannot, at present, unload a cargo ship, stock a store shelf, run a clean election, handle parental complaints at a school board meeting, pass a budget bill, treat a cold variant, keep order in the streets, defeat a third world country, or even evacuate said country cleanly. And that's to say nothing of all the things it *should* be doing, that all non-joke countries do, that it refuses to do. If our ruling class has a plan, it would seem to be to destroy the society and institutions from which they, at present, are the largest – one is tempted to say only – beneficiaries. Do they think they can benefit more from the wreckage? Or are they driven by hatreds that blind them to self-interest? Perhaps they're simply insane?

Whatever the case, couple all this unprecedentedness with all this incompetence, and going long on Wokemerica seems a sucker bet. But, to end where we began, the very unprecedentedness of our situation means that all bets are off.

The Birth, Benefits & Burden of Western Citizenship

Victor Davis Hanson

W HAT HAPPENS TO a society when the pernicious ideas of an elite filter down to the masses, and the proverbial people sense the foundations of their own citizenship crumbling? When crime spikes, infrastructure erodes, airliners lack fuel to reach their destinations, borders become irrelevant, tribalism returns, and Americans lose confidence in their own elections and the wisdom of their Constitution, the most likely ultimate cause of such apparent systems collapse can be traced to an erosion of citizenship.

The assault on American citizenship

The current American national malaise and dread of collective decline display a variety of symptoms. One is a sense that the middle class is weakening. Another is that America's southern border is becoming meaningless. Citizens also fear that woke identity politics are fueling a recrudescent precivilizational tribalism that threatens to endanger their lives and unwind the nation.

More formally, a vast and growing body of unelected functionaries now exercises more power over citizens than do elected officials. Credentialed elites across the professions are actively seeking to enfeeble or discard significant elements of the Constitution and the accompanying customs and traditions of nearly two and a half centuries. Self-described overseers wish to subordinate national interests and sovereignty to a higher globalist cultural allegiance and authority. All these diverse challenges still share a common denominator in the systematic destruction of what used to be called American citizenship.

Take the middle class, the traditional linchpin of consensual government. Until recently, middle-class Americans had suffered from decades of stagnant incomes, even as the country at large was affluent as never before. Middle-class and poor students owe $1.7 trillion in aggregate college debt. That staggering sum is an indictment of the pernicious marriage of federal government subsidies of and guarantees to higher education. That nexus has indentured an entire generation without providing them in return the civic education and common skills and knowledge so necessary for active and vigilant citizenship. And most observers concede that these unfortunate debts simply cannot be paid back by those who incurred them.

The percentage of Americans owning homes – the modern equivalent of the founding ideal of land-owning and empowered citizens – is again declining. The average net worth of Americans at retirement is also plunging. About 40 percent of American adults can only make minimum payments on their mounting credit-card debt. Such stagnation occurs at the moment the federal government is borrowing trillions of dollars for the greatest array of redistributive entitlements in its history.

All these statistics have consequences for the nation as a whole. The ages at which Americans marry, have their first child, or buy a home have risen to new highs. American fertility rates reach new modern lows. The native-born population of the United States shrinks and ages. In circular fashion, once middle-class viability erodes, an ever-expanding government is asked to subsidize Americans in vain attempts to provide some of the entitlements that citizens once confidently earned themselves.

The result is the very government-induced dependency about which the nineteenth-century Americanophile Alexis de Tocqueville once warned: an ennui of prolonged adolescence replacing the pride and dynamism of the self-reliant citizen. From the time of Aristotle, political scientists have warned that consensual government cannot endure without the majority of the population transcending the dependency, volatility, and subservience of the poor, while also circumscribing the reach of an entitled, self-interested, and often disdainful elite. In a reductionist sense, the middle-class citizens, unlike the aristocracy and plutocracy, do not seek to win profitable government concessions. And unlike the poor, they do not depend on state redistributions.

Equally important for democracy is a sense of place, a common landscape in which American citizens are free and feel secure to craft their own culture and protect their laws and customs – without constant foreign threats, demographic pressures, and migratory challenges. What is true of America is true globally: Western civilization is at the crossroads. Without demarcated and fixed borders, citizenship becomes impossible. It devolves into a slew of contradictory and warring castes of alien residents, guest workers, and migrating tribes, each demanding the privileges of the legal citizen while claiming exemptions from his responsibilities. Citizenship's values become diluted when no one knows precisely where the frontier ends or begins, and thus whether a particular farm, hamlet, or town is or is not protected by and responsible for a consensual government. A cacophony of languages confuses national allegiances, and overtaxed social services are the inevitable result when millions migrate across an open border and compound their first illegal act with a second of residing in a foreign country without permission.

An estimated twenty million foreign residents currently remain in the United States illegally. Over the present fiscal year, nearly two million foreign nationals are forecast to enter the United States without legal authorization. Most will likely cross the wide-open southern border unvaccinated and untested for COVID-19, while Americans are warned that their government may go door-to-door to roust them out for inoculations. Yet without borders, we return to the scenarios of the Dark Ages of tribal migrations, when entire shadow populations vied with citizens for claims on the land, without any desire to acquire the language, customs, and traditions of their hosts.

America's once-successful melting-pot approach to integrating, assimilating, and intermarrying legal immigrants has not been so much replaced by a "salad-bowl" alternative of primary allegiance to separate identities as it has been by sheer chaos. Millions of immigrants vote with their feet for better lives in the United States. Yet their American hosts increasingly have little idea why that is so, and none about how these migrants might rapidly become fellow citizens. The current faddish term of the moment – "woke" – is simply a new word for the ancient idea of tribalism, of destroying a citizenry's common affinities and primary loyalties to a consensual government and replacing them with elemental kin ties and prejudices based on superficial appearances, shared languages, or religious zealotries.

Such tribalism – the incendiary stuff of ancient empires, as well as the former Yugoslavia, Iraq, and Rwanda – supersedes mere hyphenated names and identity politics. Race, not class, is considered the more immutable demarcation and therefore becomes a desirable and useful divide.

Certainly, the civil rights–era dream of Martin Luther King, Jr. – our character, not the color of our skin, is what matters – is increasingly challenged by a new reactionary wokist creed that to fight bad discrimination, one must embrace good discrimination. Or to put it another way, to curb racial obsessions, one must first become obsessed with racial differences. Few reflect that a large multiracial democracy is history's rare, fragile, and volatile artifact, or that until recently America was about the only nation in history that had even tried such an ambitious project.

The diminution of the middle class, the porousness of our borders, and the proliferation of the dangerous idea that race is essential, not incidental, to who we are – all these occur almost innately. It is as if America itself is reverting to a premodern, precivilizational region, or a territory of peasants and residents, rather than a modern, industrial nation of empowered citizens whom the free world relies upon.

Yet, simultaneously, there are more deliberate and coordinated efforts of elites to curb or replace citizenship. Call them the postmodern bookends to our premodern forces of civic erosion. The unelected bureaucrats at the state and local levels now number in the millions. Recent scandals, controversies, and incompetencies within the alphabet soup of federal bureaucracies – at the CDC, NIH, IRS, DOJ, DOD, FBI, and CIA – share one common feature. Unelected but powerful federal employees often have infringed upon the rights of citizens to be free from government surveillance, from government hounding, from government warping of their private tax information, from government appropriation of constitutional freedoms, from bureaucratic alterations in their elections, and from infringement of their constitutional protections.

All these challenges to democracy are not new but a part of all historical governments. They were even common during the vast growth of the ancient Athenian bureaucracy, in the various governments residing at Versailles, and in both the czarist and Soviet Kremlin. Yet consensual societies, by their very equality-minded social and economic ambitions, are the most prone to creating an always growing bureaucratic state of "helpers." All democracies and republics eventually suffer the appropriation of power by the unelected in the legislative, judicial, and executive branches of government. When one functionary has the combined power to make laws through edicts, then to adjudicate whether they are legitimate, and finally to enforce them with the power of the state, then there is no longer a free and consensual government.

Aside from the insidious unelected bureaucrats, there are more systematic and deliberate revolutionaries who seek to alter citizenship as envisioned by the Founders. These are often supposedly the nation's best and brightest legal minds, social activists, and elected officials. Yet the revolutionary progressives breezily talk of ending the 233-year-old Electoral College, the 180-

year-old Senate filibuster, the 150-year-old nine-justice Supreme Court, and the sixty-year tradition of a fifty-state union – all revolutionary changes predicated on the hope of a vice president breaking a fifty–fifty tie in the Senate. These are merely the first agendas of those who also now question why senators are not proportionally elected as are those congresspeople in the House of Representatives and state legislatures, or why Supreme Court justices are not subject to periodic referenda as is true of many state appeals-court justices, or why ranked-choice voting is not used uniformly in federal elections as it was recently, for example, in the Democratic Party primaries for the New York mayoral race.

Common to all these multifaceted attacks on the way America has been governed is the leftist idea that our customs and laws never had any legitimacy, whether constitutional or legislative, given they did not result in an equality of result. Rather they supposedly reflect an endemic failure of government to ensure "equity" – the radical egalitarian idea of mandated equivalence that overrides all individual differences in ability, talent, energy, luck, and character.

The First Amendment has long been under assault by social-media monopolies and on campuses. Various schools of "critical legal theory" now argue that law enforcement, arrest, and prosecution should be selectively predicated on social, economic, and racial criteria rather than on legal statutes. When mayors, governors, and police chiefs cannot stop the mounting epidemic of inner-city violence, they blame the Second Amendment. Yet illegal, unregistered, and often stolen handguns or edged weapons – not so-called assault weapons – account for over ninety percent of all murders. On campus, constitutionally protected due process of those accused is selectively applied, depending on the political nature of the charge. Crying "hate speech" or "sexual assault" so often results in the suspension of all constitutional guardrails, as campus administrators vie to signal their righteousness as judge, jury, and punisher. In some sense, progressives now fear and loathe the First Amendment as much as they traditionally despised the Second.

There are other elite challenges to American citizenship. No nation has a longer history of uniquely stable constitutional government than the United States, not the ancient civilization of China, not Russia, not one in Europe. Yet economic globalization is now often conflated with envisioned global political harmonization, as if the natural expansion of quasi-free-market capitalism ensured the worldwide adoption of constitutional governments and thus like-minded national tesserae in a one-world mosaic.

Our current Secretary of State, Antony Blinken, invited a so-called "racism expert" from the often-illiberal United Nations to audit America's allegedly spotty record on race and equity. International commercial accords are predicated not on symmetry, but persist in operating under the sclerotic assumptions that unfair free trade with America was necessary for nations to reboot a stagnant post-war world. Global and Westernized elites at Davos currently talk of a future "Great Reset" in which nations adopt top-down reforms of their economies, determine their energy use according to transnational norms, and adopt global guidelines on everything from corporate governance to reparatory diversity policies.

Civic education, ancient American customs, and popular shared traditions are rejected as toxic because they are not perfect. Few acknowledge that the glue that held together an otherwise chaotic, unruly, and once-tribal America was composed of shared national and religious holidays, our collective respect for American icons, emblems, and traditions, and the appreciation of the reasons why most immigrants head for the United States while few Americans leave for homes elsewhere.

In sum, without a popular allegiance to a viable middle class, a defined and shared space with secure borders, and a common identity of being an American that transcends our particular tribes, there can be no citizenship. Nor can citizenship survive if our elites entrust its maintenance and protection to the millions who are unelected and unaudited but often invisible and powerful. Citizenship also will disappear if a few seek to alter the Constitution or change time-tried customs and traditions for ephemeral political advantage. And the American idea of governance and its ancient traditions will fade if forcibly synchronized with global trends.

Strangely, Americans often assume that their inheritance as citizens – entitling them to vote and hold office, to enjoy free expression, and to have freedoms protected by a 233-year-old Constitution – is commonplace, both now and in the past. Yet citizenship in a consensual society is not even the global norm today. Only about half the world's individual nations even claim to be constitutional republics or democracies. And citizens were even rarer in the past.

The origins of Western citizenship

Civilization – as distinct from citizens and citizenship – began prominently seven thousand years ago with the birth of settled, urban, and stratified populations in the Near East and Mesopotamia. Intensive, irrigated agriculture allowed surpluses of labor and capital to be diverted to building cities, forming organized militaries, and establishing laws. Two millennia later, even more complex civilizations birthed still more sophisticated cultures in India, China, the Nile Valley of Egypt, on Crete, and throughout the Aegean. All these cultures mastered monumental temple-building, sophisticated record-keeping, and highly developed art.

Yet none of the first civilized dynasties and monarchies had any notion of citizenship, at least as we might now describe it. Subjects, peasants, and serfs could not vote on the laws they were subject to. Nor could they elect their own officials or audit their rulers. Free speech and autonomous courts, judges, and juries simply did not exist. The ability to craft monumental cities depended mostly on the coercive organization of labor and farming.

There is striking engineering brilliance evident in the pyramids at Giza (*ca.* 2600 B.C.), the Cretan palaces at Knossos and Phaistos (*ca.* 1600 B.C.), and the tholos tombs at Mycenae (*ca.* 1400 B.C.). But these centrally planned civilizations were largely organized from the palace by monarchs and theocrats. Even among those who were not legally defined as slaves, there was little idea that those who farmed or fought for a Mycenaean king, Egyptian pharaoh, or Cretan lord had any say over how, when, or why. Writing, as in the law code of Hammurabi (*ca.* 1750 B.C.) or the Linear B inventories from Mycenae (*ca.* 1450 B.C.), was mostly confined to administrative edicts and the inscribed *res gestae* of the rulers. It is salutary to study these early preclassical civilizations, as well as those in China and India, and marvel at their scientific progress and their development of written scripts, but none of them evolved into what we would now call a constitutional or consensual system.

Note that Western citizenship rarely had much, if anything,

to do with race. Elsewhere to the north and west, poverty and tribalism predominated among Germanic and Gallic tribes. Most of present-day Europe was then sparsely populated, the haunts of warring tribes from the Atlantic to modern-day Ukraine. Descriptions of such "white" peoples in Caesar's *Gallic Wars* and Tacitus's *Germania*, while sometimes romantically condescending, are mostly Roman ethnocentric deprecations of tribal savagery beyond the Alps, Danube, and Rhine. "Freedom" (*Freiheit*) is a word of Germanic origin that originally reflected a natural wildness rather than the ability to retain liberties within a complex and often urban environment. Migrating tribal peoples could do as they pleased only because of an often-empty countryside – and not due to the later impulse of *libertas* in classical citizens to be free from the overreach of a ubiquitous state. Civilization's more difficult task, then, was to define and protect a citizen's rights within a stationary, literate, and complex society.

Citizenship proper, however, arrived late in history, and at first only among a small number of people in the isolated valleys of rugged Greece. After the final collapse of the Mycenaean Greek palatial civilizations in the twelfth century B.C., and the gradual ascendence out of the four centuries of the subsequent depopulated Greek Dark Ages, something quite strange in history appeared in eighth-century Greece. A novel idea of a more decentralized and consensual civilization emerged among some 1,500 small Greek city-states or poleis. Despite periodic dalliances with authoritarianism, the tyrants, strongmen, aristocrats, and monarchs in these communities were increasingly forced to share governance with a broader emerging land-owning class.

Why such a singular and unprecedented change? We are not sure. But population growth; increased emphases on intensively farmed grains, grapes, and olives; the rise of armored infantrymen or hoplites; and the well-protected and isolated valleys blessed with a Mediterranean climate all seemed to combine and become force multipliers of a growing agrarian middle group.

These emerging citizens were intent on protecting their new-found private property from confiscation and curbing burdensome taxes. The reality that residents could congregate most of the year outdoors in good weather facilitated frequent mass assemblies of most of the voting population, in a way impossible, for example, in northern Europe.

Unlike the subjects and serfs of prior dynasties, the city-states invented the idea that at least half the residents who owned small farms had the unique right to say what they wished. They won the privilege to elect their own officials and to vote on their taxes, budgets, and when to go to war. Their equal seats in outdoor assemblies were mirror images of their slots in the infantry phalanx. Both reflected the agrarian grid of small farms outside of town. The city-state ethos reflected natural equality rather than a top-down enforced equity.

This new economic autonomy fostered political independence. City-states of stationary peoples insisted on demarcated borders – often marked by formal boundary stones in addition to natural rivers and mountain ranges. Inside them, unique laws, customs, and traditions united the citizenry of the particular polis for generations. Borders made Thebans distinct from their Athenian neighbors, and both from the vale of the Spartans. Borders encouraged civic solidarity and security. Ancient familial loyalties slowly atrophied once a defined space had united disparate tribes. The Greeks relegated their pre-city-state past to vestigial chauvinistic myths and replaced such clannish bonds by shared fealty to constitutional states.

Statesmen were wary of popular pushbacks if they changed civic rules for temporary advantage. Unelected officials were necessary, but when they grew too numerous and intrusive were blasted by comic dramatists and rhetoricians. No one comes off worse in Aristophanes' comedies than the lifelong politician or busybody bureaucrat. Enlightened Socratic philosophers of the more sophisticated and wealthy city-states talked of Greeks grandly as "citizens of the world" ("cosmopolitans") well beyond the Aegean. But rarely were these dreamers given the reins of government to reify their sketchy utopianism. Philosopher kings remained the stuff of Plato's utopianism.

By the late sixth and early fifth century, the result was a spate of monumental temple building, an expansion of the Panhellenic Games, the canonization of epic and lyric poetry, the emergence of natural philosophy, and the beginnings of drama, history, and sophisticated scientific inquiry. The fragile Hellenic achievement of citizenship was brilliantly defended and enhanced at the battles of Marathon, Salamis, and Plataea, in the face of the successive invasions of the overwhelming forces of the transcontinental Persian Empire. It turned out that citizens who could determine their own fate could also fight more effectively than those who could not.

In such a diverse geography as Greece there were, of course, exceptions to the city-state model – as there are today with nations outside the West. The large, rich plains of Thessaly and Macedonia clung to Dark Age horse cultures of monarchy and hereditary aristocracies rather than pursuing intensive homestead farming.

Sparta solved the dilemma of its growing population and finite land by conquering the fertile plains of nearby Messenia and much of Laconia – and reducing their populations to serfdom to produce food under coercion. Sparta's atypical but vaunted infantry largely grew out of an internal police force necessary to monitor a large population of restive helot serfs and indentured food producers. And the more the crack security forces of Sparta scoured the southern Peloponnese to put down internal unrest, the more they were away from home – and the more the legendary but tenuous Spartan fertility was endangered.

Soon, however, there arose concerns over combining consensual government with free markets and private property – paradoxes all too familiar to us moderns. Century-long political debates arose in the abstract among the philosophers such as Pythagoras, Plato, and Aristotle and often led to civic strife, graphically recorded by the historians Herodotus, Thucydides, and Xenophon.

Challenges to early Western citizenship

How, citizens argued, can a society retain the ideal of equality when natural differences in individual talent and industry, bad luck, or varying degrees of health all work against equality of result? Was freedom then always at war with an unnatural equality of result that required undue state force to sustain it? Was it then better to have the citizens roughly equal in perpetuity but equally less prosperous and less free?

As broad-based oligarchies began in many regions to evolve into democracies, where property qualifications eroded, more radical assemblies became untethered from past customs and constitutional parameters. Plato joked that the vote at Athens would eventually be extended to the animals of the polis who could logically complain that otherwise they were, unfairly, less equal than others.

When officials are elected, and laws and policies are made by majority votes, the Greeks wondered, who are the adults in the room that remind hoi polloi to save money for the future? Can anyone ever remind democratic voters that there is no paternal abstract "they" to take responsibility other than themselves? And when a democratic people without constitutional guardrails votes to do what it wishes on any given day – enslave or kill the Melians, send a democratic fleet to attack democratic Syracuse, or execute the admirals at Arginusae recently responsible for a stunning naval victory – is that a reflection of popular will or mob frenzy?

Citizens of democracies damned landed oligarchies as inevitably corrupted by rich insiders, with too many outsiders left out of power. Landed traditionalists in turn retorted that those unstable democracies pandered to the appetites of a supposedly ignorant mob and were capable of anything – and everything – at any time. Rome eventually felt it could solve these Hellenic dilemmas by fashioning a compromise, a representative republic of elected officials who would craft laws rather than allow mercurial citizens to vote directly on policies. The Roman Republic borrowed freely from the more conservative Spartan and Cretan constitutions in establishing checks and balances among what we call now the legislative, judicial, and executive branches.

As Romans studied the supposed abuses of Athenian democracy, they became energized to check the popular abuse of power. They settled on two consuls rather than one yearly chief executive and allowed tribunes of the "people" to exercise "veto" power over the wealthy and aristocratic Roman Senate. Most importantly, Rome initially saw that their system naturally required material prosperity and broad security to enable the time-consuming chores of self-governance. Early on Romans mastered the challenges of creating networks in all types of weather, leading to brilliantly engineered roads, aqueducts, and drainage canals to bring in clean water and dispose of sewage, as well as urban police and fire departments, and laws conducive to commerce. The material success of the Romans and the longevity of both their republic and empire had a profound effect on later generations of statesmen in the West, who more often emulated the pragmatism of Roman governance than the volatility of the radically democratic Athenian model. The American Founders assumed likewise that consensual government could not exist without a prosperous citizenry that in turn requires the sanctity of private property and the opportunity offered by a free-market economy.

Other contradictions of earlier Greek citizenship posed similar dilemmas for republican Romans. Who could be a citizen? Did citizenship require one to look Roman, to be native-born, or to speak Latin? The Romans eventually concluded that the Greek city-states had become ossified and static, never developing into a Panhellenic nation, because they lacked the mechanisms to incorporate and assimilate talented resident aliens, who often were more industrious than natives. Romans learned to be more inclusive by assimilating non-Romans and then non-Italians as citizens. By the third century A.D., Roman emperors and those in the ruling classes were occasionally not even native Latin speakers.

Rome had transformed the idea of citizenship into more of a creed of common values and traditions than a requirement of similar ethnicity and appearance. *Civis romanus sum*, "I am a

Roman citizen," as Cicero pointed out in the waning republic, soon became a badge of honor and a guarantee of privilege throughout the Mediterranean. Citizenship, not just the look of being Italian, was what gained respect and concessions. And yet, as the empire grew and aged, and non-Romans wished for the protections of Roman citizenship without its responsibilities, the population regressed to regionalism, sectarianism, and ultimately tribalism. What had once brought success unwound and in opposite fashion ensured decline.

Unlike other imperial efforts, originally Roman culture and civilization had spread in ways that superseded its deadly legions. Romanity initially sought to assimilate and integrate conquered Gauls, Spaniards, North Africans, Asians, and eastern Europeans, who acknowledged that their newfound privileges of clean water and sanitation, the legal rights of habeas corpus, and protections from tribal violence were at least no worse than their own indigenous alternatives.

Yet more paradoxes arose as the Roman Republic transmogrified into world government. Within an integrated intracontinental economy, Romans reached unprecedented levels of affluence. But how then were citizens to retain their ancient agrarian virtues and respect for materially poorer past generations, central to republican government, when material paradise seemed in reach on earth?

Free markets had not just accommodated the burdens of consensual government but unfortunately spawned a pernicious *luxus* – what today we might call luxury to the point of decadence. Read Petronius's brilliant first-century A.D. satirical novel *The Satyricon* to sense how the spiritual descendants of once-hardy rural Italians had fallen into gluttony, sexual debauchery, ennui, and sloth on the Bay of Naples. Roman *luxus* is presented as the catalyst of decline in the late-republican and early imperial literature of Catullus, Tacitus, and Suetonius, as well. The eventual answers to this dilemma of the deleterious dividends from an efficient global economy and stable governance were sometimes thought to be found in imported religious sects, most prominently a radically new Christian idea of the Sermon-on-the-Mount virtues of abstinence and poverty – or at least the idea of not fully indulging the appetites when to do so was both legal and materially easy.

Slavery was endemic to all ancient societies and exists in hushed pockets today in areas in Africa and Asia. The Islamic world enslaved as many Africans as did Westerners, who throughout the Mediterranean and eastern Europe were themselves often enslaved by Islamic Ottoman armies and Mediterranean pirates and buccaneers. Prior Greek debates over chattel slavey and its contradictions for a supposedly consensual society of free citizens were *never* resolved, at least in the sense of a singular Western end to what was universal throughout the world.

In the Western Roman Empire, the insidious and pernicious system of slavery persisted against occasional criticism, perhaps because it was never fully identified with race rather than with the endemic misfortunes of war or birth, and, equally, because the idea of leisure was seen as a necessary requisite of participatory government and civic education. That is, there was no state investment in the pseudoscience of racial superiority and thus, paradoxically, no embarrassment when slaves so often proved smarter and more industrious than their masters and thus more deserving of citizenship. Meanwhile, enslavement for some was self-servingly defined as necessary for the enhancement of freedom for others. Roman slave owners might shrug that they kept slaves because they had the power and desire to do so – and needed no supporting dogmas of either their own ethnic superiority or of natural servile inferiority. When anyone in theory could become a slave, slavery then became an equal-opportunity hazard. And by the same token, a potter in Athens who frequented the ecclesiae and law courts did so on the assurance that his slave was busy at work.

Throughout classical antiquity, there was a constant class war between the haves and have-nots, resulting frequently in horrifically violent revolutions. But the idea that government was created by citizens and thus could be adapted to enhance the opportunities of the oppressed, and the notion that free markets and private property made those inside the boundaries of a city-state or republic more prosperous than those outside, tended for a thousand years to prevent civilizational suicide.

The rebirth of citizenship

Given all these successes, why then did this classical experiment with citizenship come to an end in the West with the deterioration of Rome, though it persisted in various strains in the East at Constantinople?

The decline and extinction of the classical world is a long story. But the answer that later Western political thinkers such as Machiavelli, Locke, Montesquieu, Gibbon, and perhaps our own Founders took from the end of classical antiquity was that it is never easy for citizens to govern themselves unless they are well-informed, civically involved, unified, and prepared to fight enemies abroad while at home working to preserve ancestral values and shared traditions.

It is not sustainable to create a vibrant free market unless the winners share some of their largesse through private civic investment, philanthropy, and liturgies – and conduct themselves outwardly in spirit as if they were still of the middle class. It is not easy for such consensual governments to defend themselves when a cacophony of voices seeks to borrow and spend now, rather than to invest and save for later crises – whether Athens's fourth-century B.C. fight over shorting military expenditures while swelling the Theoric Fund that subsidized public entertainment and festivals, or America's accrual of nearly $30 trillion in debt at a time of spiraling entitlements and waning defense readiness. Declining fertility, a debased currency, a politically weaponized military, an ignorant and indifferent citizenry, and resurgent tribalism were often cited by Roman contemporaries as the catalysts of Western decline once the ancient virtues were forgotten. Affluence, then, as the Roman poet Catullus warned, could be a greater threat to consensual governance than poverty.

So, citizenship was for a time mostly lost after the end of classical antiquity. The ensuing poverty, insecurity, and depopulation of the European Dark Ages conspired to make it nearly impossible to resurrect. Yet centuries after Rome, empowered citizens gradually reappeared sporadically in medieval Britain, Renaissance Italy, the western and northern Europe of the Enlightenment, and among the colonies of North America – always amid more numerous tribal, autocratic, and dynastic enemies.

The American Founders knew well the classical origins of their experiment with a constitutional republic – and its long, episodic, and checkered history – which served them well in their own revolutionary era. They worried about existential challenges all around. The rich too often felt they were wealthy because of superior breeding or divine blessings, and thus deserved exemptions found under monarchies and hereditary dynasties. Meanwhile, tribalists insisted that natural affinities lie first with those whom they looked most like. Clerks and scribes assumed that their intimacy with the gears and levels of government should give them the right to ignore the will of the people.

Too many abstract moralists whined that since constitutional government proved not perfect, it was simply no good. Theocrats lectured that the divine should rule on Earth as well as in Heaven, while utopians felt their superior systems of governance could be stretched thin across the globe. The West has suffered all such challenges to citizenship during Hellenistic and Roman imperial times, the post-Roman Dark Ages, the Inquisition, the Napoleonic Wars, the two global conflagrations of the world wars, the carnage of Hitler, Stalin, and Mao, and an often-chaotic current world.

Almost alone, the new American Constitution sought ways to ensure that the small property–owning, commonsensical classes remained the bulwark of the new nation. In emulation of the success of the classical world, Americans built into their new system of governance innate ways to change and question the status quo, in the singular Western tradition of self-criticism and reexamination.

For all the subsequent dislocations of the vast frontier expansion, the Industrial Revolution, the Civil War, two World Wars, the Great Depression, the suffrage and civil rights movements, and the cultural revolutions of the 1960s, America did not just endure, but became the freest, wealthiest, and most powerful nation in the history of civilization. Key to that miracle were the resiliency of American citizens and the rights and responsibilities entailed in that citizenship.

Americans are correctly confident people that enjoy the oldest continuous democracy on the planet, one that is the foundation for the wealthiest, most free, and most secure nation in history. But with such power and privilege ought to come not just responsibilities, but humility and some anxiety over the fact that our experiment is *not* the normal custom of the current world and never was in the past.

The enemies of citizenship are usually more numerous than its friends. And no democracy or republic survives if its participants come to believe that it always will, without need of collective sacrifice, tolerance of dissent, constant reinvestment in the middle classes – and knowledge and forbearance of their own past.

The West that Wasn't

ANDREW ROBERTS

*As for the West, it is a land of sleep; darkness weighs on the
place where the dead dwell.*

TAIMHOTEP
funerary stela, *ca.* 45 B.C.

*Un homme qui dort tient en cercle autour de lui le fil des
heures, l'ordre des années et des mondes.*

MARCEL PROUST
À la recherche du temps perdu

LAST NIGHT, I awoke in a feverish state. Looking around,
I was quickly put right. The books on my nightstand were as I
had left them; the armoire hadn't moved. But for however long
I had slept, I was visited by what I now realize are horrors of a
sort unimaginable by the waking mind. What was so gruesome,
in hindsight, was how real it all seemed. The world was not populated by aliens or demons. Instead, my mind served me a buffet
most recognizable, but simultaneously *off.*

Let me provide a taste. In my dream, an atlas informed me
that I hailed from a country called Rus, not England, and in my
pocket calendar a flight by plane to the United States had become a

balloon trip to a place named Biru. Only after careful investigation did I determine I was living in the present day and not some other, since that calendar was dated not *anno Domini* but according to the "Coptic Era" (for which the abbreviations were "c.e." and "b.c.e."; it was a happy coincidence that both calendars centered on the same year). My checkbook had disappeared, as a centralized state jealous of private property had outlawed banks and private lenders some time ago. In its place I found an account of gold stores and livestock in my possession, apparently remitted to me by the imperial authorities. Dazed, starting out into the street, I hailed the first passerby I saw and asked where I might find a doctor; he scoffed at the luxury, which he said was reserved for the Rus elite, and bade me follow him to the community sauna. In short, this was a version of the world in which the West had lost, or more accurately, never come to be. Kipling advised us to not make dreams our master, and so I haven't. Nonetheless, my trip into the uncanny may prove useful in ascertaining our present real-world ills.

This is not to say that my counterfactual vision was entirely without pleasure. Indeed, counterfactual history can be a delightful pursuit apart from its obvious danger. Which professional scholar has not at times been tempted to play Horus, nudging the possibilities of chance to elaborate alternative and potentially convincing versions of the past, given the mercurial concatenations of circumstance that determine our mapping of the *then* to the *now*? This, it seems, is what my mind did while I slept, indulging in the game of speculative historiography. I wonder whether my nightmares were brought on by general trends in academia. Scholarship in the last few decades has aimed at "decentering" or even "decolonizing" the received narratives of our history. While the facts of the past that we possess remain obstinately the facts, my mind sought to play tricks on me, perhaps inspired by the malignant sorcery of our academic paladins.

It was, indeed, only by the stubborn irruption of reality – flashes of truth even my sleeping imagination could not ignore – into this ghoulish narrative that I was able, on awakening, to disabuse myself of its falsehood and fancy. What follows, then, is my account of a world we can be glad not to inhabit – and if traces of the world we do inhabit, counter-counterfactuals of a sort, have recurred and insinuated themselves therein, I have let them stand as markers by which the absurdity of my dream might be judged. For if absurdity is a poison, the antidote comes from the same source.

As Ulysses says in Shakespeare's *Troilus and Cressida*, "Take but degree away, untune that string,/ And, hark, what discord follows! Each new thing meets/ In mere oppugnancy." This principle was at work in my dream, and the string became untuned early, never to be put right. The event that set the wheels in motion was the Battle of Actium of 31 B.C.E. (that is, "Before the Coptic Era"), which was won by Cleopatra, who defeated her rival, the Roman general Octavian.[1]

Alas, this is to get ahead of myself. History moves forward, but its study must be conducted in retrospect. My vision of Actium and what followed could not but cast its antecedents in a new light. That is to say, my mind sought explanations for its inventions in prior fact. It needed a running start, on firmer ground.

---

1   In reality, Octavian won, assuring Roman dominance in the Europe of the time and the cultural ascendancy of Roman precedents thereafter.

And so it drifted back almost five centuries before Actium, to the defeat of Athens by Sparta in the Peloponnesian Wars, which saw the remaining nine vessels of the Athenian fleet escaping, eight to Cyprus, one to Athens to deliver the bad news, after the battle of Aegospotami in 405 B.C.E. The former Athenian empire was now definitively rid of the system of government known as "democracy," which Cleisthenes had briefly imposed and Pericles had extended and exposed to the ambitions of competing states, a contest that resulted in Athens's absorption by Alexander the Great in 338 B.C.E. Alexander arrived six years later in Egypt, where he founded his eponymous city, which of course remains the seat of the Papal See to this day.

After the great conqueror's death, it was Ptolemy of Lagos who gained the satrapy of Egypt in 323 and was proclaimed king there in 304. The annexation of Lower Nubia by Ptolemy II supplied three major advantages upon which the subsequent members of the dynasty founded their dominance: African war elephants, the gold reserves of Nubia, and access to the west and central African iron-smelting works already present in the region for a millennium. The completion under the Ptolemies of the Suez Canal, along the same route as the excavations of Darius I of Persia in 500 B.C.E. (which in turn followed a route which dated back a potential further thousand years), established Egypt's trading dominance on the routes to India and in the lands that later became the empire of Mali.[2]

The fortunes of the Ptolemaic dynasty and the simultaneous

2　The "Canal of the Pharaohs," the predecessor of our modern-day Suez canal, was in fact completed in the time of the Ptolemies but closed down in 767 A.D.

ascent of the Roman Empire during the following three hundred and fifty years naturally held a key place in my somnolent account of civilization, but for the present purpose we must now move forward to the confrontation between Cleopatra and Octavian in 31 B.C.E. The Queen of Kings had been proclaimed twenty years earlier, and her sexual liaisons with Julius Caesar and his successor (and her consort) Mark Anthony left her perfectly positioned to take advantage of Octavian's overweening ambition.

After the assassination of the first Caesar, the Roman domains were divided between Anthony and Octavian, the former taking the east and the latter the west. Octavian's fatal gamble was his attempt to present Anthony as a traitor to the Roman cause when in the Donations of Alexandria he divided the eastern empire between Cleopatra, Caesarion (her son by Julius Caesar), and Alexander Helios and Ptolemy Philadelphus (Anthony's own offspring by the queen). Collectively, their apanages comprised Egypt itself, Cyprus, Cyrenaica, Syria, Armenia, Parthia, Phoenicia, and Cilicia, thus much of the known world beyond Italy and Western Europe, then in the thrall of Rome.

Anthony may have been less skilled a general than he was a geographer, and the military historians of my dream remained divided as to the extent of the risk Cleopatra ran when, with her legendary boldness, she engaged her warships at Actium. Anthony's fleet of broad, heavy *quinqueremes* had given battle to Octavian's lighter, more maneuverable *liburnian* boats for several hours without result when Cleopatra, who held her forces in the rearguard, gave the signal for retreat. Anthony was unaware of the ruse. In the confusion that followed the apparent retirement of the Egyptian vessels from the field, Cleopatra divided her fleet and pressed around her ally's flanks, bearing down on Octavian's ships from either side and funneling them within range of Anthony's archers.[3]

It was, as the counterfactual historian Barry Strauss notes in his new book, *The War That Made the Roman Empire: Antony, Cleopatra, and Octavian at Actium*, the "hinge" of history.[4] We might call it the crossroads of civilization. Strauss presents a captivating tale of what *might* have been had Octavian and Agrippa won at Actium over Anthony and Cleopatra. "Actium," he notes, "was the decisive event, and its consequences were enormous." Had the battle turned out otherwise – had Augustus won, the center of gravity of the Roman Empire would have shifted westward. Rome might well have won out over Alexandria or Byzantium as the capital city of the ancient, and later our own, world. The world would have spoken Latin, not Greek. Strauss imagines the monument Octavian might have raised to commemorate his victory:

---

3   Historians agree that Anthony and Cleopatra faced long odds in attempting to escape from the Ambracian Gulf, at whose mouth the city of Actium was located and within which Octavian had pinned their naval forces. As Barry Strauss explains in *The War That Made the Roman Empire*, we cannot know Anthony's precise strategy, but it was probably known to Octavian, thanks to the last-minute defection of Quintus Dellius, a top commander from Anthony's camp. Cleopatra and the Egyptian reserves nevertheless succeeded in breaking through Octavian's lines, near the center; joined by Anthony and perhaps a few other ships, they sailed for Africa with their war treasury on board. They left over half their ships and the vast majority of the Roman legions behind. There were minor skirmishes afterward, but two centuries later the Roman historian Cassius Dio was not far off in asserting that the decisive victory at Actium gave Octavian "sole possession of all power" in the Roman empire.

4   Strauss's book is, of course, entirely factual. *The War That Made the Roman Empire: Antony, Cleopatra, and Octavian at Actium*, by Barry Strauss; Simon & Schuster, 368 pages, $30 (March 22, 2022).

The Victorious General [*Imperator*] Caesar, son of a God, victor in the war he waged on behalf of the Republic in this region, when he was consul for the fifth time and proclaimed victorious general for the seventh time, after peace had been secured on land and sea, consecrated to Mars and Neptune the camp from which he set forth to battle, adorned with naval spoils.

But it was not to be.

The niceties of Cleopatra's strategy have provided topics for many pleasant scholarly gatherings, but the outcome is undisputed. Cleopatra's ships sailed into harbor at Alexandria dressed for victory. When news of their triumphant return reached Octavian, who was trying to augment his depleted troops in Syria, the great-nephew of Julius Caesar fell upon his own sword with the words, "I wished to be Augustus; so ends the West." What may have seemed at the time vainglorious appears to have been borne out by the events that followed.

Cleopatra had Octavian's body brought to Alexandria, where it was interred with appropriate honor beside that of her unfortunate husband Anthony, whose death from an asp bite coincidentally occurred on the very evening of Cleopatra's coronation as the first Ptolemaic Emperor of the Romans.[5]

---

5   The biographer Plutarch tells us that Anthony committed suicide in Alexandria on August 1, 30 B.C., after a false report, possibly sent by Cleopatra herself, that she had done likewise. Cleopatra in fact killed herself nine days later – the story goes, by putting an asp to her breast.

Over the next six hundred years, the Ptolemaic Empire flourished, in counterpoint to the slow death of the former Roman dominions to the West. Alexandria was already established as the intellectual and cultural center of the world. Though its vast and unparalleled library suffered collateral damages during Julius Caesar's siege of the city in 48 B.C.E., the collection was soon restocked with some 200,000 volumes from the Pergamon book hoard, which represented one of Anthony's last gifts to his Egyptian queen and which are still consulted by scholars to this day.[6]

A list of Greek-speaking scholars whose discoveries in the library at Alexandria further advanced Ptolemaic civilization must include Euclid (geometry), Archimedes (engineering), Aristarchus of Samos (the heliocentric concept of the universe), Eratosthenes (geography, the circumference of the Earth), the doctors of the Hippocratic tradition (nervous, digestive, and vascular systems of the human body), and Callimachus (cataloguer and etymologist), yet the language of the Eastern Empire was also developing in train with another great innovation, the introduction of the Coptic Church established by a mystic named Mark on his arrival in Alexandria in 42 C.E. As the monastic system introduced by the Coptic Church spread across the lands of the Ptolemies, so too did learning, medicine, and succor for the poor. The other significant figure in this tradition was Pope Arius, the leader of the Coptic Church who in the late third century infused its theology with a radical humanism that would, ultimately and blessedly, affirm the validity of pagan worship.[7]

---

6   The only counterfactual aspect here is the assertion of the library's longevity: in reality, intermittent pillaging and general neglect had reduced it to a shadow of its former self by the time Saracens took Alexandria in 640 A.D., destroying what remained.
7   The Christian heresy of Arianism, which held that Jesus was not co-eternal with

THE WEST THAT WASN'T

The spiritual toleration that had been so important an aspect of Alexander's conception for Egyptian society (as evidenced by his insistence on preventing his troops defiling the animal necropolis at Saqqara with their presence) was realized as the Qubt language of the Coptic Popes melded with demotic Egyptian, Greek, and Latin and was made manifest in the tolerance of each individual's deistic preferences. Some continued to worship Isis and Horus, others transferred their hope of salvation to the demi-gods Mark and Arius, still others adhered to the pantheon of the Greeks, but none within the apanage of Alexandria were persecuted.

What a contrast to Rome, the exhausted former champion of Europe! In the aftermath of Actium, those inhabitants of Latin Italia with any pretensions to ability or ambition made their way as soon as possible for Egypt. The population that remained, over time demographically dominated by former slaves, endured a slow leaching of their military and cultural certainties under pressure from incursions from the Germanic tribes, whose fear of the legions had once restrained them beyond the Rhine.

In its long and painful death throes, the Roman Empire behaved with a viciousness that sadly became all too typical of the barbarism that followed over nearly two millennia. It is an interesting footnote to history that only antiquarians know of, but around 33 C.E. the Roman provincial governor of Palestine, Marcus Pontius Pilate, actually crucified an unknown Jewish carpenter-rabbi on no better grounds than the suspicion that he might be a

---

God the Father, was stamped out by the Council of Nicaea, convened by the emperor Constantine in 325 A.D.

troublemaker. (This crime, long blamed on the local populace, was in fact the fault of the Italians who ruled the province rather than the powerless Jews who lived there.) From what little we know of the anonymous rabbi's teachings, mainly from the apocrypha of various colleagues and followers of his decades after his death, modern scholars have apprised a fine and decent man with a number of uplifting liberal messages, but sadly his cult died with him on a hill outside Jerusalem.[8]

Ironically enough, the very absence of booty in the former realm of Octavian protected the rump of the Roman Empire from cataclysmic attack. Put simply, by the time of the great earthquake that destroyed what remained of the Colosseum and the other mighty monuments of the former imperial city in 443 C.E., there was very little left worth looting.[9] The colonies of Hispania and Gaul gradually returned to their earlier customs and cultures, while the island of Brython, having been briefly inspected by Julius Caesar, remained quietly on the edge of the map and gave trouble to nobody. The Druids there, whose descendants claim ownership of Stonehenge and regularly use it for religious festi-

---

8   In reality, the consolidation of the Roman Empire by Octavian, which paved the way for the extension by later emperors of Roman citizenship to those living in the territories, was also a necessary precondition for the flourishing of Christianity. As Harry Jaffa explained, when "everyone was a Roman, then Roman law was everyone's law. The separate gods of the separate cities had been the lawgivers of their cities. If there was but one law there must be only one God. Some form of monotheism was thus destined to become the Roman religion.... Christianity was able to combine the monotheism of Judaism with the universality of Roman citizenship."

9   The source of this earthquake was finally correctly attributed to the fault in the Monte Vettore range by seismologists investigating the tremor that further blighted this corner of the world in 2016.

vals today, appear to have been the most impressive of the Bry-
thons almost until modern times.[10]

Tribal, hierarchical, patriarchal, vicious, and constantly feud-
ing, the peoples of Western Europe spent much of the Dark Ages
(*ca.* 31 B.C.E.–1850 C.E.) in backwardness and ignorance in com-
parison with the rest of the world. Life there really was, in the
words of the Wessex-based political philosopher Thomas Hobbes,
"solitary, poor, nasty, brutish and short." There were some exceptions to this overall tale – Cambridge University, the Abbey church
of Woden in Londinium, for example, and the cathedral of Our
Lady Cleopatra in Chartres – but nowhere could the term "civilization" really be extended to the West except perhaps for Moor-
ish Spain after the assassinations of Ferdinand and Isabella in 1492
and Ottoman Vienna post-1683, and in both places the inability
of Islam to reform internally also led to suppuration and decay.[11]

The advent of Islam – which, after the decline of Judaism,
became the sole remaining Abrahamic religion – in Arabia from
the mid-seventh century onwards heralded the division of the
Ptolemaic kingdoms and their eventual absorption by the great
Caliphates that constitute the essential territories of the modern
Dar-al-Islam, a vast *ummah* stretching from the Atlantic Ocean
to the gates of Indo-China. The highest point of their civilization
today is perhaps illustrated by modern-day Kabul, where until
recently the Taliban has strictly enforced sharia law, ensuring

10 The remains at Stonehenge date at least to the third millennium B.C., well
before the Celtic peoples and their leaders (known as Druids) arrived in Britain
(likely after 500 B.C.).
11 The failure of the Ottoman siege of Vienna, which lasted two months, marked
the beginning of the end of organized Muslim incursion into Europe.

that some 50 percent of the population is kept rigidly away from any activities that might increase GDP.

Simultaneously in the sixth century, the Vikings, whose homelands in Norway, Denmark, Finland, and Sweden had previously enjoyed sparse contact with the Roman Empire, began their series of explorations west to Vinland and Helluland and east to the Russias. A recently excavated settlement at the tip of what is now known as the Albinonic Fringe attests to Viking presence before 1020, though what staging posts or settlements they established were soon abandoned.[12] They did not, however, leave without learning of a practice which was to become crucial to the enduring dominance of Rus.

Those people whom the Vikings termed "Skraelings," the inhabitants of the lands west of the fringe, had long employed the sweat-lodge, or "sauna," for social and spiritual practices.[13] Though there exists considerable debate about the matter, it may be ascertained that the custom of women giving birth in such saunas existed in Finland some time before the establishment of a Viking outpost at Anse. The hygienic consequences of the sauna were, quite simply, revolutionary. Indeed, it is arguably thanks to the sauna that we in Rus, Nubia, and the Dar-al-Islam today enjoy our high average life expectancy of fifty-two years.

Thanks to the sauna, puerperal fever was eliminated in a generation and women no longer died in such tragic numbers in childbirth and consequently could provide many more children

---

12 L'Anse aux Meadows sits at the northern tip of modern-day Newfoundland and was settled by the Vikings in the early eleventh century.

13 "Skraelings" were the native inhabitants encountered by the Vikings upon their arrival in Greenland.

for their husbands and tribes. Their offspring were more likely to survive and in turn to produce healthy babies, producing an increase in population – the well-known "Viking Surge" of the eleventh century – which not only increased agricultural production but also spurred the impetus for trade. As a result of such increases in medical knowledge, today's Western Europeans only die of smallpox, polio, typhus, the Chinese bat-plague, typhoid, bubonic plague, malaria, and yellow fever.

To the east of their original dominions, the Vikings' search for amber, furs, minerals, and – somewhat regrettably – slaves saw them imposing tribute on the Chud, Slav, and Ves peoples. According to the *Povest' vremennykh let* (*The Rus Primary Chronicle*) they had by the year 852 raided as far as the Sea of Marmara, overrunning the city they knew as Miklågard, a Ptolemaic provincial capital which spanned both shores of the Bosphorus.[14] While the reaction of the Coptic Pope Photius was understandable – "Why?' he moaned, "has this dreadful thunderbolt fallen on us out of the farthest north?" – the Ptolemaians successfully resisted this first Viking incursion by dint of a new technology developed in the seventh century.

Known as "Holy Fire," this mixture of saltpeter and petroleum was sprayed through skin hosepipes from the city walls over the enemy. And though Miklågard eventually did indeed become part of the state of Rus, Holy Fire, when combined with Chinese gunpowder, has proved one of the most effective and refined weapons at the disposal of the global East, and remains so to this day. (That is not to say that others have not tried in recent years

---

14 "Micklågard" is the name given in the Icelandic sagas for the "big stronghold," which is to say Constantinople, modern-day Istanbul, which Viking travelers visited.

to advance military technology, against the will of the gods, as the summary execution of Wilbur and Orville Wright for their heresies against the order of nature attested.)

While the Vikings were extending the borders of Rus to march with those of modern-day Indo-China, the Empire of Mali – which had come to dominate the remaining territories of the Ptolemies that had not been absorbed into the Dar-al-Islam – was simultaneously extending its own trade links to the lands of the Aztecs and Incas, collectively known as "Biru." Of all the innovations discovered by the Malian merchants, the most significant was the earthquake-proof architecture these societies had perfected, which, in conjunction with the search for oil to convert into petroleum to produce Holy Fire, encouraged the northward push by a combined force from Mali and Biru into the lands of those "Skraelings" first encountered by the Vikings in Helluland.

By the year 1550, therefore, the world was thus divided into five great empires: Rus, Greater Nubia, Indo-China, Dar-al-Islam, and Biru, with Western Europe a cultural and economic backwater contributing nothing of value to mankind. This brings us to the period conventionally (though increasingly controversially) known by its Danish nomenclature, the Renæssance. The achievements of this period and its contribution to the competitive advantages enjoyed by the "global East" include, though not exclusively: mathematics,[15] gunpowder,[16] moveable metal type,[17] historiog-

---

15 Known in Egypt from 2,700 B.C., including unit fractions, multiplication, division, composite and prime numbers, and linear and quadratic equations.
16 Discovered in China ca. 850 A.D.
17 In Korea, dated definitively to 1377 A.D. with the completion of the earliest

raphy,[18] and linear perspective.[19] We might add paper money, nautical innovations such as the rudder and separable bulkhead, and the blast furnace, the two former from China, the latter from Greater Nubia.

The decision on behalf of the Five Empires to ban usury, for fear that it might encourage the development of what counterfactualists call "free markets," saved the world from many dangerous innovations over the centuries. Any danger that there might be an industrial revolution in the West was effectively snuffed out by the *ukase* against borrowing and lending, with the obviously beneficial results that the West retains its largely barter economy that is so popular today. The danger posed by the limited joint-stock company, by which individuals banded together to pursue entrepreneurial activities, was ended once the Batavian authorities clamped down hard on the practice in the early sixteenth century.

Similarly, popular obscurantism and rules against absurdly over-optimistic adventurism kept the West safe. Although few outside the academy have ever heard of him, in the late fifteenth century there was a Genoese adventurer called Christopher Columbus who was fortunately unable to raise the capital necessary for his harebrained schemes of sailing westwards to the Indies.

The arrest and execution without trial of Galileo Galilei in April 1633 might seem harsh half a millennium later, but at least it put paid to the outrageous and ludicrous notion that the Earth revolved around the Sun, which if adhered to by enough people

---

extant moveable type–printed book, *The Anthology of Great Buddhist Priests' Zen Teachings.*

18   Attested by tenth-century A.D. Indian commentaries on the *Raghuvamsa*, an epic poem dating to the fifth century A.D.

19   Employed by Li Cheng of China, who died in 967 A.D.

would undoubtedly have led to a great doubt among the populace of the verities of our present-day existence.[20] Galileo paid a
high price for his heresies, but times were much harsher then.
Our knowledge that the Sun moves around the Earth – and the
banning of any teachings or experiments to the contrary – keeps
Western society happy and contented.

With regard to punishment, today the stonings and decapitations
in Dar-al-Islam stand out as exceptional, whereas the rest of the
world is far more civilized; for example, the late Ronald Reagan
only had his thumbs branded by the Dublin Consistory Court
when he wrote his illuminated manuscript promoting such ancient
Attic notions as "democracy." Considering the absurdities he
attempted to promulgate in the 1980s – a belief in rationalism,
individual liberty, freedom of speech, the rule of law, and so on –
it was extraordinary that he got off so lightly. Fortunately, there
seems to be no one on the present political scene who has followed his heretical lead.

Indeed, we can be proud of what the world has achieved since
Cleopatra's glorious victory at Actium. There have been occasional moments of violence – the burning at the stake of Leonardo
da Vinci and Michelangelo for innovative artistic expression was

---

20 In truth Galileo was arrested and tried for these beliefs and forced to abjure by
the Catholic Church in 1633. This fact is hardly a credit to the Church's tolerance,
but the reality diverges from the above counterfactual in two important respects:
first, that instead of being killed, after his conviction the aging Galileo retired to his
farmhouse in Arcetri, Italy, until his death in 1642; and second, that the public nature
of the trial, predetermined though its conclusions may have been, and the private
records thereof have afforded subsequent generations the opportunity to form their
own opinions about the authority exercised and the degree of justice attained.

of course regrettable, though probably necessary – but overall the absence of what counterfactualists call "liberal values" has strengthened Western society to the point that average wages there equate to over forty groats a year after tax, enough to buy two bullocks and eleven goats. This is meaningful wealth. Meanwhile, Western arts and culture have been confined to the graceful whittlings of the eighteenth-century woodcarver Antoni Stradivari and the musical experiments undertaken with Chinese nose-flutes by Wolfgang Amadeus Mozart and Ludwig Beethoven, who both hailed from the Viking-occupied region of Germania.

We have already noted the health revolution instigated by the sauna. Whether it was the Skraelings or the Vikings who were responsible for the origin of this technology is a continuing source of debate. The same ownership issue holds true in the case of the technology that permitted the unification of the innovations listed above and resulted in the definitive dominance of the "global East": the balloon. Whether one subscribes to the theory that balloon travel was developed by the Nazca peoples of the pre-Inca Biru, or to the contending argument that smoke balloons were built and tested in twelfth-century Yin China, it is undoubtedly the case that the dissemination of the knowledge of the Renæssance was the consequence of air travel. The fact that it is now possible to fly from Kiev to Machu Picchu in a mere eight and a half days is incontestable evidence of the efficacy of the vehicle which truly revolutionized the world.

This account has, notably, left out most of what we in the real world call "the West." But what account could I give of such desolation as inhabits the Albinonic Fringe, these balloon "flyover states"? Just as the early Vikings passed over the desolate wastes of Brython and Gaul in their pursuit of plunder, so too must I neglect and dismiss the contribution and potential of these regions to our global historic narrative.

But then I began to stir. Earlier in the dream, the characterization of the inhabitants of the Fringe as backward, pale, flabby, beer-swilling primitives only fit to dig for coal seemed justified. Even accepting their early advances in chariot technology and thatched architecture, the sophisticated trade between Brython and Gaul, a coinage system, and their richly decorative shrines, temples, and tombs, it seemed to me that such people deserved their backwards reputation. But then more doubt crept in. What if the current gatherings of senior tribesmen in Brython known as *witans* shows a potential for representational government similar to that which was cast out of Athens more than twenty-five centuries earlier? Yet I shook it off, rolled over, and returned to my dream. It is clearly absurd to believe that a democratic system could ever take root in places like Brython, where so little of note has emerged from the mists for over a thousand years. Back dreaming, it became clear to me that democracy remains as yet too delicate and dangerous an idea to be released to the mercies of the masses. For such an idea genuinely to work, we would need centuries of civilizing institutions in the West to instill such concepts as the equality of men and freedom of conscience, and of course there was no prospect of that happening even in the distant future. Instead we must be content with the exciting new developments taking place in Kabul, in the easternmost part of the Dar-al-Islam Empire, where women have occasionally been allowed to leave their houses unaccompanied by their male relations, and the local Council of Islamic Scholars has, in its infinite mercy, banned women from being beaten with canes wider than a man's thumb. The world is therefore on the correct path, and is undoubtedly a happier, richer, and better place without the dangerous and revolutionary concepts of democracy and Western civilization.

And then I awoke. Over my morning coffee I reflected on this alternate universe, one in which the glories of Western civilization were not, instead, achieved by the East but, in fact, not achieved at all. While contemporary scholars may decry the West's past, attributing to it all the ills that continue to bedevil our imperfect world, my dream showed me a world without the West: no protection against serious infectious diseases; no six-hour transatlantic flights; no real knowledge of what occurs beyond Earth's atmosphere – the list of technological liabilities goes on and on. In some ways, the political and social penalties are even starker. For congregated under the word "democracy" are all manner of signature Western achievements, from the ideal of equality before the law, the protection of private property ("the first object of government," according to James Madison), and the cultivation of free markets, to the Socratic spirit of self-criticism and open debate. Let us not blindly praise the past, but nor should we denigrate it without just cause or proper context. Historians who chide the bad but ignore the good leave many gaps for invention, something scholars and citizens both present and future would do well to remember.

The Indispensable Country

CONRAD BLACK

THE CURRENT MOMENT may seem to be a crossroads. Western civilization may either continue to lose its apparent competitive superiority over its chief rivals, or it may reaffirm its enduring status as the principal influence in the world. But those outcomes have always been possible since the initial rise of the West. Once the West, including in particular the Middle East, began organizing itself into governments approximately six thousand years ago – earlier, as far as can be determined, than in what is now India and China – there was no rival to Western civilization as it progressed, plodding and lurching, through the centuries. The age of exploration and discovery, which came quickly on the heels of the rise of the nation-state in the fifteenth and sixteenth centuries, effectively rendered the European powers unchallengeable as the most advanced civilization in the world, particularly in science and technology. And the European nationalities then peopled the Americas and a large part of Australasia, permanently establishing themselves as the principal demographic presence in the world and on three and a half of the six populated continents.

The West also asserted the right to take over the administration of South Asia, the balance of Australasia, Southeast Asia, almost all of Africa and South America, and, at the end of the First World War, much of the Middle East. By the end of the Second World War, the Japanese Empire was included in the Western hegemony. The thought of there being any competing civilization in a position to force the West to a crossroads has only arisen in the last thirty years with the swift economic and scientific ascendance of the People's Republic of China. This arrival of China as an alternative leading influence in the world to the West, and specifically the United States, was made possible by the adoption by the totalitarian Chinese government of a capitalist system, though a state-directed one. (This, despite the Chinese government's professed communism.) The Chinese challenge was facilitated by the propagation of the theory, after the disintegration of the Soviet Union and the collapse of international communism in 1991, that history had reached its apotheosis and that Western democracy and the free market were now unbeatable as a method of governmental, societal, and economic organization. (Francis Fukuyama was the chief exponent of this view.) And the rise of China to a state of apparent rivalry with America and the West was accelerated by the general Western view that concessions to China would be received as encouragements to adopt altogether the Western model of government and economics that had just won the greatest and most bloodless strategic victory in the history of the world with the disappearance of the USSR.

Threats foreign & domestic

The West is not threatened by spontaneous disintegration and collapse like many previous civilizations, though there are times when watching the nightly news could incite that fear. The crossroads under discussion are whether the West is about to be surpassed by the Chinese, and whether for the first time in history the principal influence in the world will be something other than, broadly speaking, a Western one. This question would not arise if the People's Republic of China had not – contrary to the hopes and expectations of Western governments – abused the generosity of the Western powers to conduct wholesale industrial espionage, manipulated the Chinese currency to produce huge trade surpluses, engaged in an extraordinarily ingenious policy of cheating and gaming the system of international agencies and regulations, and violated international waters and boundaries to claim a hegemony over a vast sweep of the Far East and Central Asia. The culmination (to date) in this vertiginous sequence of provocations was the outrageous but brilliant improvisation, after the novel coronavirus apparently accidentally escaped from a Wuhan laboratory, of unleashing the virus on the world while ruthlessly trying to stamp it out within China. China has reaped the competitive benefits of the West's harebrained comprehensive economic shutdown and diluvial expansion of its money supply, which was meant to compensate the scores of millions of people pitchforked out of work by their governments in their panic-stricken response to the virus and has resulted in widespread inflation, among other doleful effects.

The contemporary spectacle of the Western world worn ragged by this interminable COVID crisis – which has been hideously compounded by the incompetence of its leaders in responding to a virus from which 99.5 percent of healthy people recover and 95 percent of those above the age of sixty-five and with other compromising afflictions do – would in itself justify questions about whether the West really is a preeminent civilization. It is far from being a solely American problem, but the American condition is particularly distressing. The more venerable among us, who have been following American affairs closely since, in my case, the Korean War, can scarcely believe the news from that country. While tearing down statues of great men, the unrestrained "peaceful protests" of the summer of 2020 killed approximately thirty people, injured thousands, and produced over $2 billion of property damage. The federal courthouse in Portland, Oregon, was attacked and damaged for nearly two hundred consecutive nights, and there were nightly television appearances by such sages as Hawk Newsome, the New York head of Black Lives Matter, promising to "burn America down" if all their egregious demands were not acceded to at once. All of this has abated somewhat; the defunding of police is being reversed in the face of skyrocketing violent-crime rates in many cities, represented most visibly by flying squads of smash-and-grab burglars gutting the showrooms of luxury-goods emporia on some of the most famous boulevards in the world. It is clear that the public is finally very concerned about the level of violence.

Even a cursory glance at contemporary America reveals a great many other disconcerting phenomena: a ludicrous secretary of homeland security robotically repeating with nodding head on one side of a split television screen that "the border is closed"; on the other side of the screen, a steady stream of people, twenty or more per minute, wades or simply walks into the country with no one even to take their names. The rate of inflation is not accurately reflected in the Consumer Price Index, and when the rising costs of gasoline, home heating fuel, bread, basic building materials, and new and used automobiles are taken into account, the real rate of inflation is close to 10 percent and rising. On entering office President Biden stopped the Keystone XL oil pipeline from Canada and ended fracking on federal land and offshore drilling where he legally could. This consigned the United States to again being a vulnerable energy importer, after the nation had taken daily oil imports down from fifteen million barrels in the Clinton years to self-sufficiency in the Trump years. This administration embarrassed America by publicly asking for increases in oil production from OPEC, which includes such rabidly Ameriphobic countries as Iran, Russia, and Venezuela.

It was painful to hear the current American secretary of state, Antony Blinken, open an important meeting with the Chinese foreign minister in Alaska with a somewhat pitiful exposé of America's alleged shortcomings; this is all the more shameful as it was before the world and to a senior member of the government of China, which is practicing a form of genocide against its Uighur minority and is persecuting all religions that are not simply mouthpieces of the central government. China is exceeding the levels of authoritarianism conceived in the imaginations, much less the experiences, of Kafka, Koestler, and Orwell and claims now to be able to identify and hunt down anyone in urban China within ten minutes. The People's Republic has effectively torn up its treaty over Hong Kong with the United Kingdom, one of the world's most respected nations and one relatively unaccustomed to such cavalier treatment. While it was practically impossible to set foot out of doors anywhere in the Western world prior to 2016 without being buttonholed by someone advising – with the deathly righteousness of an evangelical Christian bellowing that the end is nigh – that China was about to surpass the United States, that tiresome practice ended altogether while Donald Trump was president. He imposed sanctions on China pending more favorable trade arrangements, increased the strength of the Seventh Fleet in Far Eastern waters, and achieved closer and more reciprocally supportive relations with India, Japan, and several others of China's neighbors. Now, the Chinese lose no opportunity to announce that they are about to become the dominant power in the world. That is a chilling thought to every other nation in the world with the possible exception of North Korea, and that is one of many reasons why it is not likely to happen. We heard similar from the Third Reich and from the Kremlin in their day. The threats are easily distinguishable, though, and China is not a greater worry.

Afghan errors

The most disturbing recent development that could incite notions of American and Western decline in both absolute and relative terms opposite China was the horrifying debacle in Afghanistan. There is little doubt that the nation-building policy adopted by the United States after the NATO and United Nations occupation of Afghanistan, following the terrorist attacks on the United States in September 2001, was too ambitious for the forces that could be justifiably deployed by the world for such a mission. Landlocked, primitive, tribally factionalized Afghanistan was judged by Britain and Russia in the nineteenth and twentieth centuries to be unworthy of the investment of people and resources that would be required to subdue and modernize that rugged, poor country. The American-led Afghan enterprise, having deposed the government of the Mullah Omar and having chased al Qaeda out of the country following the 9/11 terrorist attacks, would have done better to effect less radical changes to Afghan life and empower elements capable of holding fast, while retaining a few bases to facilitate counter-terrorist activity if it became necessary. In a particularly unfortunate example of mission creep, the United States and its allies effectively shouldered the task of dragging that terribly backward country uphill into the twenty-first century, to no particular good purpose other than distant altruism, which is not a cause in pursuit of which the United States and the West have the means to be too extravagant.

The conduct of the new Taliban government in its first four months of renewed office reflected the economically desperate condition of Afghanistan and the fact that more than half of the population of the country was born in the twenty years since the West occupied it. There have certainly been outrages, but not remotely on the scale of those committed by the former Taliban regime that came after the unsuccessful 1979–89 Russian invasion of Afghanistan and subsequent civil war. The Trump administration recognized the hopelessness of the mission as it had evolved: the attempted complete modernization of Afghanistan supervised by token forces of under ten thousand armed personnel representing all of NATO. Trump managed to avoid American casualties for the last eighteen months of his administration with a firm understanding that the United States would indeed be leaving. His position was strengthened by a refusal to depart under unacceptable conditions and his demonstrated willingness to strike with great severity at militant Islamic leadership, as he proved in killing the head of the Iranian terrorist apparatus, Qasem Soleimani, in January 2020 after Iranian-prompted attacks on the U.S. embassy in Baghdad.

It had become a very unsound mission, as Iran, Pakistan, India, Uzbekistan, and other powers had their own Taliban factions active in Afghanistan, and the NATO presence had become too small to assure the retention there of any Western values. The public life of Afghanistan was sustained only by fears of Western, and particularly American, reprisals if their forces were attacked. Access overland into Afghanistan was through Pakistan, and Pakistan was using American military aid to bankroll a leading Taliban faction in Afghanistan that frequently attacked American and allied personnel. It was an impossible situation, but that did not justify what occurred under Biden. With no consultation of allies who had loyally invoked NATO's Article 5 to contend that the attack upon the United States on September 11, 2001, constituted an attack upon all NATO members, and that all NATO members should join the United States in responding to it, the United States announced a swift, effectively unilateral withdrawal on a tight schedule. Contrary to all logic and experience, instead of evacuating all vulnerable personnel and troops in a logical sequence – logistical and support workers first, down to the most mobile and easily extracted forces last – the world witnessed a shocking fiasco that recalled the pitiful people clinging to the undercarriage of American helicopters as they evacuated Saigon in 1975. Over a hundred thousand Afghans were airlifted out without much regard to their credentials for requesting such a rescue. Meanwhile, an unconscionably large number of those who had been closely identified with the allied effort were left to face the wrath of the returning Taliban. Also abandoned was $85 billion of new military hardware. This is not what confident great powers do.

In August 2021 the British Parliament declared its contempt for the president of the United States, albeit informally – an unprecedented step. (During the American Revolutionary War, General George Washington was referred to in Westminster as a traitor but never with contempt.) Throughout the life of the Western

Alliance, now nearly seventy-three years old, America's allies have disagreed with the United States at times, but they have never before questioned its military capability or the competence of its military commanders. They quite justifiably did so in respect to the Afghanistan operation. Precipitate American decline was suggested by irresolution and incompetence at the highest civilian and military levels. The defense secretary, General Austin, and the chairman of the Joint Chiefs of Staff, General Milley, lamely explained the failure of the U.S. Army and Air Force to devise and execute a professional and effective policy. They and other senior officers disputed, under oath in Congress, President Biden's claim that no one had advised him of how quickly NATO's protégés in Afghanistan would collapse. Somehow the president described this shameful flight as "an extraordinary success." Milley's further admission that the United States was behind both China and Russia in the development of hypersonic missiles and did not have adequate defenses against them and that a recent test of such technology by China was a "Sputnik moment" was a further attestation that senior officers have been preoccupied with imbecilic micro-examination of the racial thoughts and gender sensibilities of their (entirely voluntary) forces, rather than with doing the necessary and the dutiful to protect the nation and its interests.

A country not imploding

To any reader of intelligent declinist scenarios, such as the works of Oswald Spengler, America may appear to present a classic case of inexorable decline: a military besetting itself with nonsensical allegations and investigations of racism and bigotry against transgender people; a border open not only to the desperate of

Mexico and Central America but also to the riffraff, the human slave traders, and the murderous gangs and gangsters of the world. America on any day appears to be a country where the national political media are almost completely dishonest and dedicated to a narrative that is constantly hyper-critical of the United States; the academy, from the corrupt teachers' unions to the students and faculty of many of the most illustrious universities in the world, inundates those that are supposedly learning with the notion that the United States is an evil country founded to preserve and amplify slavery. Wall Street, Silicon Valley and its oligarchic social media–platform cartel, Hollywood, professional sports – all of these are, by any reasonable criteria, anti-American. The pillars of finance and captains of industry are cowardly tools intimidated by any threat of a boycott and apparently willing enough to claim that any dissent from electoral laws that require verification of the integrity of the ballot (which the great majority favors) is tantamount to Ku Klux Klan–dominated segregation, even slavery itself. No sensible person could dismiss out of hand the argument that such a country is unfit to lead the Western world and is no match for so highly motivated and purposefully directed a superpower as the People's Republic of China. But the United States is not in fact imploding.

Every country has its mythos, and that of the United States is among the most vivid and strenuously propagated of any. When it was a new country, the lore was mainly of the future rather than of the past. The Americans were the wealthiest category of British citizens prior to the American Revolution and were principally represented by Benjamin Franklin in London. They, and Franklin in particular, agitated successfully for the British to expel the French from Canada, where they posed an intermittent threat to the safety of the colonists in New York and New England. In doing this, Great Britain almost doubled its national debt, (£74 million to £134 million). At the end of the Seven Years' War (the French and Indian War), as the expense of the war had largely been incurred on behalf of the Americans, it seemed only fair to the British government that the Americans should pay the same additional tax, especially the Stamp Tax, that their British cousins were already paying. This was a grievous tactical error: the British had no ability to collect an unpopular tax in America, and the goal for which the tax was imposed had already been achieved. If they had levied that tax on the Americans before embarking on the Seven Years' War (into which, in America, the British were precipitated by the overzealous actions of then-Adjutant George Washington in 1753, when he ambushed a French detachment overlooking what is today Pittsburgh), it would have been accepted happily.

In one of the great diplomatic *tours de force* of world history, Benjamin Franklin, having helped persuade the British to evict the French from Canada, twenty years later almost single-handedly persuaded the French king and government to assist the Americans in expelling the British from their American colonies. France's desire for revenge on Britain was understandable, but its willingness to go to such lengths on behalf of republicanism, democracy, and imperial secession was a grievous self-inflicted wound that contributed materially to the fall of the French monarchy starting with the attack on the Bastille six years after the end of the American Revolutionary War. Unlike almost all the other established Western nations, the new United States did not have a language of its own. Even small countries like Sweden, Denmark, the Netherlands, and Portugal had their own languages and distinguished literatures. The United States had a much smaller population than the British Isles and was thus a distant second among English-speaking countries, but it boldly staked out its position as a universal nation, a democratic meritocracy, a place where all (non-enslaved) people were welcome and all could rise as high and as quickly as they wished and were able.

Like every national mythos, it was in some measure a scam, not only for the reasons tiresomely recited by leftist historians and revisionists such as Howard Zinn and much of current American academia, loudly amplified by the nasty morons in the self-hating American media and Hollywood. The Americans had no greater liberties after the Revolution than before; what they had was a resident government. They had no greater civil liberties than the British, Swiss, Dutch, or populations in much of Scandinavia. But they had already demonstrated the astounding sense of show-manship that has never deserted the United States and that reached its highest – or at least most universally accessible and persuasive – point with the motion picture, television, and enter-tainment industries. It was great showmanship as well as soaring eloquence that led Thomas Jefferson, on behalf of his fellow slaveholders and the rather avaricious Boston legal and business community who spurred the Revolution, to proclaim in the Dec-laration of Independence that it was "self-evident" that "all men are created equal," and that the United States of America consti-tuted a unique human experiment in the pursuit of liberty. This was in some respects true, eventually. The indictment of poor old King George III was bunk, but it was resonant.

The self-evident nature of Jefferson's egalitarianism was not well demonstrated in the subsequent constitutional compromise according to which the states allowing slavery received representation in Congress equivalent to their free population plus three-fifths of their unenfranchised slave population. Nor did the somewhat louche conduct of the Sage of Monticello himself – with his alleged fathering of six children with his slave Sally Hemings – give much credence to the idea. Franklin started as a slaveholder and ended as head of the Abolitionist Society of Pennsylvania. Washington emancipated his slaves in his will; Jefferson called slavery "a fire-bell in the night." They all knew it was a terrible moral problem, and in the end America's greatest leader would promise:

> If God wills that all the treasure piled up by the bonds-man's two hundred fifty years of unrequited toil shall be sunk, and that every drop of blood drawn by the lash shall be repaid by a drop of blood drawn by the sword, then as was said three thousand years ago, so it must be said that a judgment of the Lord is true and righteous altogether.

Abraham Lincoln was going to abolish slavery no matter how many white men died doing it (perhaps 750,000 did so, of a total Union and Confederate population of about thirty-one million; there was nothing mythical about the human cost of the Civil War). The protracted but ultimately determined commitment to integrate America on a basis of full racial equality is unrivaled by any comparable national effort to raise up a subjugated racial minority to a position of equality. That is why the claims of contemporary black militants are unacceptable and will be rejected, including by the great majority of blacks.

There are other problems with the traditional American mythos, and the United States has arrived at a stage when these vulnerabilities are being exposed. This is not entirely an undesirable development – so extraordinary is the success of the American project, it no longer needs much of a mythos; the facts are persuasive. The exaggeration of America's shortcomings by its internal enemies does not reduce the astonishing accomplishments of the American nation: in two long lifetimes, from the end of the American Revolution to the end of World War II (1783–1945), the United States advanced from several million citizens and three-quarters of a million slaves clinging to the North American Atlantic coast to the nation that possessed half of the economic product of the war-ravaged world. America maintained an atomic monopoly and won immense admiration and prestige for its role as the principal liberator of much of the world from the unspeakable crimes of Nazi Germany and its collaborators and the scarcely less widespread and uncivilized bloodletting of the imperialist Japanese. At the starting point, the American Revolution, the world took note of the brilliance of the colonists' leaders: Washington, Franklin, Hamilton, Jefferson, Adams, Madison. And 162 years later, as the United States established within its own borders the United Nations, for which there were high hopes at first, America's civilian and military leadership was approximately as distinguished: Franklin D. Roosevelt, Truman, Eisenhower, Marshall, MacArthur, Nimitz, Acheson, Kennan, and others.

Like every other nation, and with less to be ashamed of than any other great power except possibly Great Britain, the United States has had its undistinguished and even objectively reprehensible moments. But no sane person can doubt its influence or its benignity. It provided the margin of victory in World War I and tried to transform that war into a crusade to end war. Woodrow Wilson inspired the masses of the world with the vision of enduring peace and international cooperation. The United States enabled the democracies to continue in the war in 1940 and 1941 and led the Allied powers to victory over the most monstrous succession of totalitarian, barbarian great-power regimes in history: Nazi Germany and imperialist Japan, and in the Cold War the Soviet Union. America was, from 1917 until 1991, the indispensable nation. Its leaders recognized that without American intervention, dark forces could control the Eurasian landmass and in particular the sophisticated economic and military forces of Western Europe and the Far East. American leaders did what was necessary to prevent the descent into what Winston Churchill described as "the long night of Nazi barbarism unbroken even by a star of hope ... made more sinister and more protracted by the lights of perverted science." No quantity of malignant, sophomoric casuistry or racist mythmaking by nihilistic street bullies – with the collusion of Quislings among the nation's elites, cowering and scheming in their boardrooms and film studios, and abetted by the lazy and subversive bosses of the day-care centers that largely masquerade as the state school systems and the morally bankrupt national political media – will shake the great majority of the American public from the consciousness of what Americans have built in their own country and what they have done for the world. America has been turbulent and often corrupt and not infrequently violent, but it remains, though its institutions are strained, a vital democracy. The Americans are rivaled only by the British in the propagation of democratic government, and by no nation in the immense prosperity spurred by their generous aid programs, their trade policies, and an over-powering example of prosperous, meritocratic democracy.

When the United States recognized the Soviet challenge and declared itself to be at the head of an alliance of the "Free World," many of its allies were autocracies and were also poor: Spain, South Korea, Portugal, much of Latin America. Ireland and Israel were poor though democratic, while Japan, Germany, and Italy were rubble heaps; Germany had not been politically successful since Bismarck (fired by the foolhardy Wilhelm II in 1890), and Japan had never had one day of democratic government. All these countries bootstrapped themselves up, but none of them could have made it as quickly, if at all, without American assistance. That the assistance was largely motivated by strategic considerations takes nothing from the fact that American policy was inspired by generosity as well as astuteness. It is one of the great ironies of contemporary times that the world owes the triumph of democracy and the free market chiefly to the United States and that it is not today one of the world's better functioning democracies.

Back to the crossroads

To return to the idea of a crossroads, the United States remains overwhelmingly the most powerful country in the world. China has very few natural resources, contains no institutions in which anyone places any confidence apart from its armed forces, and is a corrupt totalitarian dictatorship. Not one utterance or number it publishes can be believed. It has several hundred million people who still live as they did two thousand years ago, and because of its absurd one-child policy, the population is aging, with a serious imbalance of males over females. Regional aggressions have alienated all its neighbors, and China is engaged in intermittent skirmishing in the foothills of the Himalayas with India. So overbearing and obnoxious were the Chinese that the Burmese colonels tolerated the recent putsch that led to the expulsion of China from Myanmar. Even Defense Secretary Austin, who is no world-beater but occasionally looks like a plausible occupant of his position, pointed out that "the Chinese are not ten feet tall." The United States is no less strong from a military perspective than it was ten or twenty or thirty years ago, and the idea of a challenge from China would not in normal circumstances be a particularly disconcerting one. As for Russia, its GDP is smaller than Canada's, and while it is a capable weapons manufacturer, it could not stand a serious confrontation with the United States. The key with Russia is to avoid facing it down so humiliatingly that it retreats into the arms of China, which would give over surplus Chinese manpower for the extraction of undeveloped Siberian resources. Any such arrangement would add a large cubit to China's geostrategic capabilities and make its challenge to the United States as the world's preeminent superpower considerably more dangerous. This nightmare will not be difficult to avoid.

The status of the West at a crossroads depends very heavily on the geopolitical health of America. India, Japan, and several of the other Far Eastern states are shaping up well and certainly are not prepared to make preemptive concessions to Beijing. But Europe is in a profound torpor: the era of the great European powers is over, and the European Union is not an unambiguous political success. It is not even competitive economically, though it is a colossal improvement on the Europe of warring states that preceded it for four hundred years. The leading European country, Germany, spends less than 1 percent of GDP on defense, is making itself a vassal of Russia in energy matters, and is addicted to trade with China. Recently it was unable to form a government even three months after its last election, since the result would be one of several three-party combinations foredoomed to a life of vacillation and tentativeness. The secession from the European Union of the United Kingdom, though it was not presented in these terms, was effectively a desertion of ambivalent Europe to seek closer relations with the United States and the old Commonwealth led by Canada and Australia: an immensely powerful bloc if it coalesces to any degree.

The United States has not fallen into irreversible decline, and what has occurred is not the implosion of the United States, the collapse of its institutions, or the sudden deterioration of its astonishingly productive workforce into a fractious, inert, and unpatriotic rabble. All of the many flippant comparisons to the decline of the Roman Empire are nonsense. When the Roman Empire was overwhelmed in the fifth century, it was three hundred years after it had reached its peak with the sequence of adoptive emperors: Nerva, Trajan, Hadrian, Antoninus Pius, and Marcus Aurelius. It was more than one hundred years after Diocletian handed away half of the Roman Empire to a coequal regime he had established in Constantinople. And it was two hundred fifty years into a period of extreme religious disunion in which the Christian elders and bishops deployed immense influence entirely independent of the emperor. The leaders of the Roman armies in the major provinces and along the frontiers had greater power and authority than the central government. Frontier defense was largely entrusted to barbarians who had been pushed into the arms of Rome by fiercer barbarians from Central Asia and whose determination to defend Rome was open to great question. Of the (depending on definition) fifty emperors between Augustus, starting in 27 B.C., and Romulus Augustulus, who was chased out as emperor in 453 A.D., thirty-seven died violently.

Rome's long sway as the greatest secular power in the known world for over six hundred years has almost no relevance to the United States. Rome was a city that gradually expanded within and throughout Italy, colonizing and generally offering security, stability, lower taxes, prosperity through pan-Italian and trans-Mediterranean trade and commerce, the elevation of serious locals to the Roman Senate, and, ultimately, Roman citizenship for the masses in exchange for the fealty of the scattered Italian jurisdictions. It took a somewhat similar approach in the major provinces, especially Gaul and Hispania, but there – and in more far-flung places and for those for whom the Italians had less affinity such as in what is now Germany, Hungary, Romania, Yugoslavia, Greece, Turkey, the Middle East, and North Africa – Rome was essentially a colonial power that enforced its will through a combination of relatively good government and instant recourse to extreme severity against the endless liberation movements that arose and were snuffed out. Rome had courts and laws and a reasonable freedom of expression; it was a respectable civic regime by the standards of the times, but again, it bears no resemblance whatever to the United States.

Rome's progress to democracy was permanently derailed when, in the late second century B.C., the great reformers Tiberius and Gaius Gracchus, who were advocating the resettling of the teeming masses of Rome to productive colonies in conquered areas, as well as some administrative reforms, were murdered by the upholders of the antiquarian, despotic rule of the factions of old Roman families in the Senate. From this point on, for a century, Rome was foreordained to be ruled by political generals who recruited their armies from the masses, paid them well from the lucrative spoils of their campaigns, and retired them comfortably by demanding pensions and allotments of territory in conquered areas for their veterans, which the Senate did not dare to resist. Thus came the succession of political generals who commanded the loyalty of their troops to themselves and not chiefly to Rome: Gaius Marius, Lucius Cornelius Sulla, Gnaeus Pompeius Magnus, and Gaius Julius Caesar. Caesar's adoptive son and grandnephew, Augustus Octavian Caesar, was a political genius who ruled with one title or another for an astounding fifty-eight years, and he devised an empire that worked well when it was directed by a great talent like himself but repeatedly fell into shambles in the hands of the less capable of his successors. (Caligula and Nero followed Augustus by only twenty-two years. This, too, has nothing to do with the United States, no matter how discouraged one might become with the Biden administration.)

Apart from the descendants of slaves, the United States is populated almost entirely by people who came or whose ancestors came to America voluntarily seeking a new life and pledged in advance to assimilate to and uphold the country where they had chosen to live. Some outrages were committed against the shabbily treated American natives who were not sufficiently numerous to resist the tidal wave of arrivals from Europe. Most black and Hispanic Americans assimilate to American life and are patriotic. They are not degenerate, undermotivated, slovenly, or surly people, and there has never in the history of the world been a workforce remotely as productive or well incentivized as the American.

CONRAD BLACK

Recent regression

What has actually occurred in the United States in the last few years, following the victory in the Cold War, was a period of over-confidence, which Fukuyama's famous essay exemplified. There followed the second time in American history when there were three consecutive two-term presidents: Clinton, George W. Bush, Obama; the previous occasion was Jefferson, Madison, and Monroe two hundred years before. Complacent administration resulted, in what amounted to a bipartisan coalition. For the thirty-two years between 1981 and 2013, one or another member of the Bush and Clinton families was president, vice president, or secretary of state, and members of both families contested for the presidential nomination of their parties in 2016. In those three presidencies, personal income growth per capita declined from over 4 percent in the last five Reagan years to a little over 3 percent in the Clinton years to 2 percent under the younger Bush to 1 percent with Obama. It was the time of the greatest worldwide economic disaster since the Great Depression, generated by the Clinton policy of requiring the majority of mortgages to be commercially unjustifiable – a political free lunch that expanded homeowner-ship and generated appreciative political contributions to the Democratic Party from the building-trades unions and the issuers of mortgages.

It was also a time of constant war in the Middle East to no good purpose: the occupation of Iraq in 2002 has vastly increased the influence of Iran in Iraq, and Iraq and Syria have effectively disintegrated. An immense humanitarian disaster of millions of ref-ugees followed. The Clinton administration conspicuously failed to take intelligence about imminent terrorist attacks seriously even after the provocations of USS *Cole*, the Khobar barracks attack in Saudi Arabia, and the bombings of the U.S. embassies in Kenya and Tanzania. The Obama administration rendered great service in showing a non-white could become president, but President Obama's chief accomplishments were the executive imposition of absurd and regressive (and ultimately illegal) curtailments of carbon emissions, Obamacare, which caused as many problems as it resolved, and the Iran nuclear agreement, which was a terrible mistake. The two parties traded control of the White House and the houses of Congress regularly, but the personnel of government was unchanged, being almost all Democrats, and the American government comfortably and complacently descended towards the left.

Donald J. Trump was an astute and flourishing developer of high-quality buildings and very successful reality television star (in a program that he conceived and produced himself). Despite a number of cheesy and hucksterish operations trading on his name – including the so-called Trump University and a Trump health plan that consisted of quarterly urinalyses and some vitamins – and a bruising interlude in the casino business in Atlantic City, he had been closely following American politics for many years. During that time he branded himself to sell the Trump name on everything from neckties and mattresses to mineral water and hotels at great profit to himself on no investment at all. He changed parties seven times in thirteen years, waiting for his moment and polling constantly. He saw 2016 as his chance. Ultimately, he translated this into high office. The bipartisan political establishment did not take him seriously; he promised to sweep them all out, and he was elected.

The appearance of American decline has not come from Trump's presidency itself, which almost eliminated unemployment, oil imports, and illegal immigration, all while compelling China to reform some of its unfair trading and monetary practices and rallying the powers of the region – from India to Australia to Japan – to concert a modified policy of containment. But his opponents were so alarmed at the Trump assault on their entrenched positions that they politicized the FBI and the senior intelligence agencies and threw a phony charge of collusion with Russia in the 2016 election and two spurious impeachments at him. The accusation that Trump had tried to foment an insurrection when some hooligans attached to a huge crowd of his supporters assaulted the Capitol – which was underprotected despite warnings from Trump and others that the Capitol Police should be reinforced – is another establishment slur. A clear indication that the United States is not in terminal decline is the vigor of the establishment response to the Trump program. The elites were not at all like the French nobility being overwhelmed by the discontent of 1789, or any other decadent ruling class, though they had become inadequately competent. Trump's opponents regrouped into a broad coalition of regular Democrats, black extremists, the Far Left, and anti-Trump Republicans. They turned a blind eye to the violence of their less presentable allies and they outspent Trump two to one and sandbagged him through the social-media platforms. They had the support of 95 percent of the national political media, whom Trump had shown in 2016 were collectively a paper tiger. For good measure, in six swing states – Arizona, Georgia, Michigan, Nevada, Pennsylvania, and Wisconsin – voting and vote-counting rules were changed with questionable constitutionality, as the Constitution requires such changes to be made by the state legislatures. The judicial branch refused to adjudicate any of the nineteen lawsuits that challenged the legality of the changes, and on this questionable basis, Trump lost the election.

The Indispensable Country

The Biden administration, for reasons summarized above, has been and is universally seen to be a complete failure, and the president himself is clearly lacking the intellectual vitality to execute his office. It seems almost inevitable that either Trump or a Republican candidate approved by him will be elected in 2024 with a clear mandate to complete Trump's work. This will eliminate any concerns about which country is the most powerful in the world, and it will assure the de-escalation of domestic political tensions and help to generate a renovation of the country's elites, who have generally failed and disserved the nation in the last twenty-five years in most fields. The spiritedness of Trump's approach and the tenacity of the establishment's defense create the appearance of a country dissolving into contumely. Five years from now, what appears to be American decomposition and decadence will be seen to have been a heavily contested two-stage national renovation.

American exceptionalism is now only a matter of scale, as many countries have better civic standards, at least equal prosperity, much better legal systems, and better functioning institutions than the United States. But they are comparatively modest-sized places and populations. America remains the indispensable country; it is not folding or waffling and will certainly not be seen off by the ugly regime in China. America is shifting gears and upgrading personnel and preparing for another mighty charge in its completely unprecedented and unrivaled rise among the world's nations. There is a crossroads in the world's affairs, but the United States of America will accelerate through it.

Going Under with the Overclass

James Panero

We don't often hear about the plight of the overclass, but our progressive elites have a problem. They have become too successful, and their success is starting to show poorly. Over the last decades, these elites have experienced the traumas of contemporary life very much in reverse to most Americans. Our difficulties have been their triumphs. Our restrictions have become their liberation. With ever greater efficiency, they have become the creditors to our debts, the marketers of our drugs, the title-holders of our homes, and the sellers of the fruits of our industry. They have risen as many others have fallen. They are good at what they do, and for this they have been handsomely rewarded. No one would deny a payment for a job well done. Yet these victories have demanded ever greater tribute from the vanquished. Progressive elites have taken their successes out on the rest of us.

America has always had its elites. For much of the country's history, American elites have been the envy of the world. Elite ingenuity drove American prosperity. Elites also returned their wealth to the public trust through their patronage of culture and medicine and their promotion of civic uplift. Their astonishing acts of generosity – to museums, hospitals, schools, libraries, parks, opera houses, and many other outlets of culture and the arts – enriched American civic life in a manner unprecedented in human history. Even the most hard-hearted industrialists understood the calling, the urgency, of these expressions of civic virtue. "All have derived benefits from their ancestors," wrote Horace Mann, the nineteenth-century American educational reformer; "and all are bound, as by an oath, to transmit those benefits, even in an improved condition, to posterity." Through the aspirations of art and architecture, through the study of great literature, and through the care for common suffering, the institutions they created – those "little platoons," in Edmund Burke's appreciation of small associations – promoted nothing less than the culture of democracy.

Americans are still the great beneficiaries of the historical largesse of this untitled nobility. The institutions that continue to enrich the country's lives are, by and large, the continuation of the ones founded a century ago or more by elite benefactors. As an expression of the importance that the American Founders placed on these private associations – for example, when it comes to the country's oldest schools – this institutional history extends to before America's national beginnings. The cultural enrichment that American elites helped to nurture has been an impressive reflection of the country's democratic ideals.

And yet, rather than support these institutions as pinnacles of civilizational achievement, many of today's elites seem determined to undercut them. They gnash their teeth at their own history. They rend their garments at their own complicity. Then they make an active show of ripping apart their charges at the seams: closing the books, covering the art, destroying the monuments, censoring the students, canceling the discourse, and ridiculing the historical mission. Such impulses inform elite behavior across the Western world. This show of cultural weakness has been a provocation with deadly consequences. For those of us still concerned with the preservation of wisdom – an inheritance of culture that transcends politics – the results have been heartbreaking. For those concerned for the fabric of democratic nations, the effects are now all the more horrifying.

A culture war by proxy

Americans find it distasteful even to speak of their elites. In a supposedly egalitarian society, the idea strikes most observers as improbable. The mere mention of an elite class can sound sinister and un-American. Compared to the Left, conservatives are even less inclined to criticize elite manners and mores, even if Tom Wolfe could be their unparalleled anatomizer. But the truth is that, far from the magnanimous elites of old, today's overclass increasingly seeks to direct what we see, what we read, what we say, and what we hear. They consolidate and monopolize. They inflate and devalue to their maximum advantage. They also tip the scales, cook the stats, stack the deck, and rig the games while championing the fairness of the outcomes. In today's meritocracy, these elites are always meant to be the best. In today's democracy, the winning candidate is always supposed to be their own. They flood people's neighborhoods, screens, and lives with destabilizing interventions. They feign concern before throwing back middle-class worries as pathologies in need of their control. The uncertainties of the many contrast with the verities of these few. And they are merciless about it. They have it figured out. They mock those who do not. Rather than lift up their fellow citizens through their charity and good will, this overclass seems determined to invalidate that common pledge, from the Declaration of Independence, "to each other our lives, our fortunes, and our sacred honor."

Going Under with the Overclass

Elite attacks are made under the banner of a mutable list of causes: social justice, climate justice, indigenous justice, trans rights, black lives, anti-racism, and so on. Tomorrow it will be a new combination and permutation of progressive politics. The shifting battlelines are a strategy of the offensive. While many of the attacks seem to originate from below, it is easy to miss the fact that the bombs have been placed, timed, and set to detonate by those at the top. It is a culture war largely waged by proxy. Today's activist elites seek to undermine the cultural legacies of the institutions they control precisely because these institutions have promoted – through their books, their art, their buildings, and their concerns for our well-being – democratic aspirations and cohesion. It is a spirit they now despise and wish to undermine.

Consider the case of Nikole Hannah-Jones. The much-discussed author of The 1619 Project would be little more than a social-media scold were it not for her platform at *The New York Times*, the company behind her publication and promotion. Despite the widely accepted debunking of her project, the "newspaper of record" has only doubled down on its initiative to undermine the legitimacy of the United States by slandering it as a slave-owning conspiracy, rather than a country that has shed more blood than any other to uphold democratic ideals. During the riots of 2020, which caused dozens of deaths, $2 billion in property damage, and untold suffering in its aftermath, Hannah-Jones wrote that it would be "an honor" for this looting to be called "the 1619 riots." She continued: "The history of non-violent protest has not been successful."

There was a time when reproducing the diagram of a Molotov cocktail – as *The New York Review of Books* did in 1967 – would be considered an act of fringe journalism. Now *The New York*

Times can read like a guide for anarchists and an apology to the criminal class. In 2017 the *Times* published an article called "How to Pull Down a Statue," which it offered under the heading of a "Tip." In 2021 it reproduced instructions by Decolonize This Place further detailing "how to take down a monument." Here it offered such advice as "For every 10 ft of monument, you'll need 40+ people" and "everyone needs to be wearing gloves for safety." It concluded: "Just keep pulling till there's good rocking, there will be more and more and more tilting, you have to wait more for the obelisk to rock back and time it to pull when it's coming to you. Don't worry you're close!" The Sulzberger family, which has controlled the *Times* since 1896, has found great profit in such stridency. As it trumpeted in its own report in 2021, the newspaper's circulation has only increased, advertising revenue is up, and its "balance sheet surpassed $1 billion in cash as it continued to build its free cash flow."

These are not isolated examples of elite behavior. Even compared to mainstream liberalism, noted Michael Tomasky, the editor of *The New Republic*, "It's an undeniable fact that Democratic Party elites, progressive activists, foundation and think-tank officials, and most opinion journalists are well to the left." Elite foundations have given over $12 billion to institutions pushing the progressive ideology of "racial equity" – as opposed to racial equality – in 2021 alone. These include the Ford Foundation ($3 billion), Mackenzie Scott (Bezos) ($2.9 billion), JPMorgan Chase ($2.1 billion), the W. K. Kellogg Foundation ($1.2 billion), the Bill & Melinda Gates Foundation ($1.1 billion), the Silicon Valley Community Foundation ($1 billion), the Walton Family Foundation ($689 million), The William and Flora Hewlett Foundation ($438 million), and the Foundation to Promote Open

Society ($350.5 million). One of the largest donors to "Yes 4 Minneapolis," the charter amendment to dismantle the city's police department, was from George Soros's Open Society Policy Center. The source for this information is not some dog-whistling outfit from beyond the pale but, again, *The New York Times*.

It should be said that many elites, perhaps a greater percentage of them, mainly see opportunity in the incendiary rhetoric. They mete out medicine based on race, for example as was done with scarce COVID treatments, while employing their own concierge doctors. They care for little beyond themselves. They are more than happy to outsource the burden of concern to the teams of progressive agonizers now on their payroll. They are also content to watch the burning. They observe the fires from a safe remove as the conflagrations never touch them. The fire-breaks, in fact, only serve to enhance their sought-out isolation. The burned-over populace only contrasts with their own glittering ascendancy. But ultimately, whether they are active or passive participants, every challenge this overclass puts out is a challenge to national legitimacy.

Elites have not given up on status. Their behavior is centered around maintaining cultural control and passing these privileges on to their heirs. At the same time, from art to architecture, statues to books, they want to break the chains of civic inheritance because these works are in a public trust that they no longer trust. In the name of national reckonings, they seek their own disunion. Inspired by this anti-democratic impulse, this revolt against the masses, today's elites promote progressive fronts to undermine national sovereignty and embitter common citizens while consolidating their own power and position.

JAMES PANERO

The betrayal of democracy

A recurring theme of these chapters is that progressive elites now drive a Western civilization at the crossroads. But just how did our highest classes become an overclass of toxic privilege? Over a quarter century ago, the social observer Christopher Lasch wrote about dangers that he diagnosed under the title *Revolt of the Elites*. Produced in his dying days, Lasch's warning came out as a feature in *Harper's* magazine in November 1994 and then as a book by Norton in 1995, this time subtitled "The Betrayal of Democracy." This challenge to democracy is the key to understanding elite dynamics. Lasch cautioned that the "chief threat" to Western culture no longer comes from an aggrieved underclass but from "those at the top of the social hierarchy":

> who control the international flow of money and information, preside over philanthropic foundations and institutions of higher learning, manage the instruments of cultural production, and thus set the terms of public debate – that have lost faith in the values, or what remains of them, of the West. For many people the very term "Western civilization" now calls to mind an organized system of domination designed to enforce conformity to bourgeois values and to keep the victims of patriarchal oppression – women, children, homosexuals, people of color – in a permanent state of subjection.

Lasch intended his title to be a riff on *The Revolt of the Masses*, the book by José Ortega y Gasset first translated into English in 1932. Ortega saw the civilizational threat of his era coming from the "mass man." Observing the births of both Bolshevism and fascism, Ortega feared an ignoble force rising up from below that maintained no obligations to history. This mass man insisted on "complete freedom." He was the "spoiled child of human history." All the while he maintained a "deadly hatred of all that is not [him]self."

Now in a "remarkable turn of events" that "confounds our expectations about the course of history," wrote Lasch, something that Ortega never dreamed of has occurred. Lasch was a writer coming from the Left. He could be too quick to denounce open markets. Some of his presentations could be vague and generalizing. But as an observer who became highly critical of the progressive culture promulgated by the new elites and their institutions, Lasch was right to home in on the class conflict that drives much of our more superficial political dynamics. Reviewing the book in *The New Criterion* in April 1995, Roger Kimball called Lasch "one of our most articulate and earnestly plangent social critics."

"The cultural wars that have convulsed America since the sixties are best understood as a form of class warfare," Lasch observed, "in which an enlightened elite (as it thinks of itself) seeks not so much to impose its values on the majority (a majority perceived as incorrigibly racist, sexist, provincial, and xenophobic), much less to persuade the majority by means of rational public debate." Ever more detached from public life and civic engagement with a full spectrum of fellow citizens, elites seek to "create parallel or 'alternative' institutions in which it will no longer be necessary to confront the unenlightened at all." The West as it exists is irredeemable, deceitful, dangerous, and in need of their elite control. The result is a class warfare waged from the top, directed down.

Lasch saw a long history of geographical sifting, "assortative mating," and other social factors as contributing to this widening social isolation and contempt. Management and labor no longer live in the same towns. Rooted industries have given way to rootless capital markets and abstract information technologies – which, we might say, now more resemble misinformation technologies. For much of America, "the decline of manufacturing and the consequent loss of jobs; the shrinkage of the middle class; the growing number of the poor; the rising crime rate; the flourishing traffic in drugs; the decay of the cities – the bad news goes on and on." Meanwhile such concepts as "meritocracy" and "upward mobility," even if pursued fairly, merely leave our "elites more secure than ever in their privileges (which can now be seen as the appropriate reward of diligence and brainpower) while nullifying working-class opposition." Through the myth of social mobility, elites in fact "solidify their influence by supporting the illusion that it rests solely on merit." The result is a "two-class society in which the favored few monopolize the advantages of money, education, and power" – results that are not only supposed to be "fair," but are now also unquestionable. "When confronted with resistance," Lasch observed, elites "betray the venomous hatred that lies not far beneath the smiling face of upper-middle-class benevolence."

"There has always been a privileged class," said Lasch, "even in America, but it has never been so dangerously isolated from its surroundings." Contempt now replaces elite obligation and noblesse oblige. "Simultaneously arrogant and insecure," Lasch wrote, "the new elites regard the masses with mingled scorn and apprehension." They now despise their countrymen, especially those who do not pay tribute to their superiority. Meanwhile,

Going Under with the Overclass

"'Middle America' – a term that has both geographical and social implications – has come to symbolize everything that stands in the way of progress: 'family values,' mindless patriotism, religious fundamentalism, racism, homophobia, retrograde views of women."

We are the virus

This elite distaste for the lower classes merges sterility with revolutionism. Where the isolation of the classes is not an option, their prescription is sanitary control: upper-middle-class liberals have "mounted a crusade to sanitize American society – to create a 'smoke-free environment,' to censor everything from pornography to 'hate speech,' and at the same time, incongruously, to extend the range of personal choice in matters where most people feel the need for solid moral guidelines."

How remarkable is it to consider that, writing over a quarter century before our pandemic closures, distancing mandates, and vaccine "passports," Lasch diagnosed the sanitizing urge of our elite culture. For all of the talk of institutional "access," more than half of black Americans, for example, were not permitted into New York restaurants, gyms, movie theaters, or museums for over a year due to vaccine mandates they did not meet. The numbers were even lower for some venues, where proof of a third shot, along with picture ID, has been required for entry. The result is that the rich are buying up all the seats, figuratively and literally, around them. Progressive elites seek to escape even the air we breathe. With great fanfare, they launch themselves into the vacuum of space and sink themselves into the isolation of the seas. And while they await their earthly escape, at the very least, they expect a double masking from their chefs, trainers, and housekeepers while they enjoy the clean air of Aspen, Napa, and St. Barts.

Ever more removed from the general population, elite life during the COVID pandemic has never been more rewarding. They have enjoyed their family camp in the Adirondacks, the river that runs through their ranch in Montana, the shifting tides rising and falling by their house in the Caribbean. Their only illness, as the saying goes, has been their ongoing bout of "affluenza." Twenty-five years ago, at the time of Lasch's writing, America's richest 20 percent controlled half of the country's wealth. As of 2021, the top 10 percent control 70 percent of the country's wealth. The top 1 percent alone controls nearly a third of the country's wealth. The top 50 percent hold 98 percent of the wealth. That leaves the bottom 50 percent with but 2 percent, a division that has only grown more stark through the pandemic as inflation, crime, and learning loss now add to the disruption. This all means that, as American cities were looted and burned, and the working classes have had nothing else to do but to mask up and clock in, a pajamaed overclass has stepped happily aside from the final requirements of democratic life. All the while, as Lasch observed, the elites "find it hard to understand why their hygienic conception of life fails to command universal enthusiasm."

The elite attack on democracy often comes out of this same fetish for sanitation. For progressive elites, structural racism, much like a viral pandemic, is a silent killer. The less you see it, the more likely you are to be already infected. Resist its treatments, and the more you are complicit in spreading its disease. You could be an asymptomatic carrier and still kill others. You could have racism and not even know it. For elite policy-makers, no treatment is too harsh, no restriction too extreme, no position too out-of-step with common sense to get to racism zero. The coronavirus response has proven itself to be merely a dry run for even greater encroachments of government surveillance and control. China continues to woo the world's elite with its permanent class of insiders, who are happy to regale their Western hosts with the siren song of benevolent, technocratic rule. Now from Europe to America, the tracking technology is in place to be deployed from one virus to the next.

Just as elites do not respect the popular vote, they do not respect the popular voice. Progressive contempt for the common man, of course, goes back more than a century. There has always been a subset of elites who, despite a purported interest in the downtrodden, are obsessed with overpopulation, sterilization, and generally advocating for "less of you and more of me." An enlightened interest in conservation, for example, has given way to the unhealthy worship of the environment and its eschatologies. The earth, the body, and the mind must now be detoxified by the same elite treatments.

"Compassionate attention, we are told, will somehow raise their opinion of themselves," Lasch wrote of the supposed beneficial effects to the underclass of a war on speech; "banning racial epithets and other forms of hateful speech will do wonders for their morale. In our preoccupation with words, we have lost sight of the tough realities that cannot be softened simply by flattering people's self-image. What does it profit the residents of the South Bronx to enforce speech codes at elite universities?" Since Lasch penned these words, elites have only doubled down on a censorious worldview that has indeed shown little profit to "the residents of the South Bronx." The gambit, however, has greatly profited elite institutions and their well-heeled class of insiders.

Diversity is their strength

Many have called social justice a new world religion. The enforcement of so-called justice over and against precedent and reason, almost exclusively a "rubbing out" of nuance rather than a "filling in," certainly conveys a religious zeal. The negative dialectics of this form of justice cannot be overstated. For all the talk of "expanding the narrative," the results always seem to be an editing down of the complexities of the human condition to the same short story of oppression. In the interest of "safety," this fetish for sanitation, this program of social justice, grants the opposite of just access. Instead it places limits on the art we can see, books we can read, ideas we can think, words we can say, votes we can cast, food we can eat, energy we can use, and people we can befriend.

A term such as "'diversity' – a slogan that looks attractive on the face of it," Lasch observed, "turns out to legitimize a new dogmatism, in which rival minorities take shelter behind a set of beliefs impervious to rational discussion." Taking advantage of America's unparalleled empathy for racial redress, this strategy of divide and conquer is nothing new. Swaths of humanity are balkanized into ever smaller splinter groups of identity factions. They are destabilized through chaotic impositions on whatever remains of faith and family. And they then have no choice but to turn to their elites to keep the peace. In this scenario the overclass is both fire marshal and chief arsonist, lighting the flames and ringing the bells.

There are plenty of true believers in this progressive faith, especially along the American coasts and in urban centers. Their politics gives meaning to their successes and justifies the failures of others. At times in America such dogmas seem to have activated a sleeper cell of Mainline Protestants – from what we might have assumed was their eternal slumber. Those held by these believers to be latter-day martyrs would have died in vain if the deaths had not resulted in conflagration. Whether the subsequent promotion of looting and "defunding" has done more than anything else to endanger the lives of poor Americans is beside the point. Elites have acquiesced to a chaos and violence that disproportionately affects the underclass – precisely the people they say they want to help. For such believers, violent purification is a justification and an end in itself. A race war, or an environmental disaster, or some other end-of-times revelation would give meaning to their dying religionism.

Few outside of elite circles, of course, hope for any of this; we would be rid of these turbulent priests and other outspoken enablers were it not for their supporters in global foundations, media, entertainment, tech, government, and finance. For them the reality is often transactional: our overclass has sold out to the highest bidder and papered it over with a diversity initiative. For the elite order, the system works. Having churned up the waters, they skim over the waves. Nowhere is this more apparent than in American education. The more uniform the school, the more it will assure you of its commitment to diversity. The more exclusive its admissions, the more we are told of its inclusivity. The more it hoards its endowment funds, the more it appeals to equity and justice. To be sure, we might still find vestiges of the "old elite" legacy clinging to these institutions. The residue of great books, great educators, and great ideas is hard to completely scrub away. Some teachers inherently reject the censorious mandates of

Critical Race Theory and the imposition of administrators in the classroom. Yet the artificial scarcity, the goosing of admission yields, the identity dogma, and the false appeals to "merit" all serve to mask the true aims of institutions that exist primarily to preserve elite privileges.

Any non-elite entrants, hand-selected by these insiders, are there to play a part in the equitable fantasy through a role not of their choosing. They are paraded in front of the banquet and are shown eating at the table. They just must obey all the directions of this legitimacy pageant until they exit stage left. For the "holiday dinner" at Yale University, for example, the freshmen are invited to a feast "decorated with holiday lights, ice sculptures, and gingerbread houses," according to the school's admissions page. "Now add eggnog, hot apple cider, prime rib, sole, roasted turkey and ham, golden potatoes, sushi, shrimp (in the shape of a Y), lobster, cupcakes, apple pie, cheesecake, fruit, chocolate covered strawberries, and a twelve-foot challah."

In December 2021, despite its own self-imposed lockdown, the school went ahead with a two-night revel. Unmasked students crowded around to record the decadence on their smart phones as, in stark contrast, a line of masked dining-hall workers could be seen pushing this "Parade of Comestibles" heaped with lobsters, lamb chops, and an ice-sculpture sleigh piled with shrimp. "The food had to go somewhere," noted Caleb Dunson, a black undergraduate and opinion columnist for the *Yale Daily News*, in a piece called "Abolish Yale," "so people started taking it by the pound. Students lined up near the meal station back of Commons, waiting to grab entire crabs and lobsters to take home with them. They grabbed turkey legs the size of my forearm and munched away at them too. We all feasted like royalty. Just two blocks away, on the city's Green, homeless people froze and starved in the bitter New Haven night."

> I left that dinner feeling disturbed and disheartened. On the walk back to my Old Campus dorm, I realized that I felt this way quite often while at this University. There's something unsettling about Yale, about the way it operates, about its very existence.... [The school's] idea of individual-driven change reeks of false meritocracy and trickle-down theory, and gives the University the cover it needs to hoard wealth and resources.

Unsentimental education

For those on the inside, the recent college-admissions scandal known as "Varsity Blues" was shocking not for its criminality but for its lack of scale and ambition. A fixer paying out bribes to the sports coaches of second-rate schools to cover non-athletic applicants is but a two-bit grift. Compare this to the subterranean pipelines that have now been laid by our elites to connect their families to the best schools, the greatest resources, and the highest potential future outcomes. There have always been elite connections. The irony is that, in this more "equitable" world, our overclass can now be just about assured of it. A high-speed rail tunnel might as well run between their child's room and the college building with their name on it. For those more problematic cases, a delta force of tutors, psychologists, strategists, and trainers is there to operate as a shadow student, providing an illusion of excellence that can seem far better than the real thing. Professionals are at the ready to do the homework, write the papers, extend the test times, shape the identity narrative, and apply to the schools. "Here is my laptop. The paper is on *Macbeth*," is how one elite tutor described a typical interaction. Some of his students, he said, had never done a minute of homework in their lives. Give an A– for such work and you will hear about it. Anything less than an A is unacceptable for such expenditures. Elite parents have all the email addresses in their assistants' files. They are not above demanding a meeting the next morning to make the grade.

There are, of course, still some old elites who hold on to the democratic faith of their ancestors as if they were Russian Old Believers. Some of the Olympian thunder we have heard from beyond the clouds concerns this fight between old and new in our board rooms, faculty lounges, and non-profit institutions. In early 2021, for example, a math teacher named Paul Rossi at New York's Grace Church, a private preparatory school, questioned a segregated racial-sensitivity training session organized by his institution. Corralled into a group of "white-identifying" students and faculty, Rossi was presented with a slide of the supposed characteristics of white supremacy. Such a list of "white" traits might come as a great insult and surprise to anyone, of any color, not versed in elite semantics, but the catechism has been making the rounds at many elite institutions. The Smithsonian's own National Museum of African American History & Culture recently presented the nuclear family, rational linear thinking, decision-making, respect for authority, delayed gratification, punctuality, and being polite all as further "signs of whiteness."

At Grace Church, the consultant asked if anyone was having "white feelings" as they looked over the list. "What makes a feeling 'white?'" Rossi asked. The school then reprimanded the teacher for "creating a neurological imbalance" among his students by questioning their racial training: "When someone breaches our professional norms," read the complaint against him, "the response includes a warning in their permanent file that a further incident of unprofessional conduct could result in dismissal." After Rossi confronted his head of school for this racialized drilling of students and faculty, the headmaster offered him a contract renewal only on the condition that he engage in "restorative practices" for the harm he had done to black students.

It is no coincidence that the traits now identified as "white supremacist" are the same ones that serve as the foundational values of democracy. Many elite schools, where day tuition approaches $60,000 a year and parents are recruited to give millions more, have become the training grounds for a post-democratic future. They will silence any diversity of viewpoint over concerns for student "safety" caused by "violent" words and ideas. The freedoms of speech, of assembly, and of conscience, as well as equality under the law, are all belittled as the values of an outdated racist order in need of elite replacement. Progressive "pain points" are then activated over the questioning of identity dogma to shuttle dissenting opinions to the door. Progressive elites are more than pleased when presented with the opportunity to winnow their ranks, sharpen their conditioning, and make examples of their apostates.

A decadent isolation

Sensing the progressive interests of today's elite universities, for which they ultimately "prep" their students, many elite preparatory schools have only redoubled their identity agenda. This is true even after a few high-profile defections: Megyn Kelly, the television anchor, pulled her children out of New York's Collegiate and Spence Schools; Gabriela Baron, a daughter of Cuban immigrants "increasingly concerned about … a de-emphasis of academic rigor and a single-minded focus on race, diversity and inclusion," did the same at Spence, where she was an alumna and trustee; Bion Bartning, of Jewish, Mexican, and Yaqui-tribe background, removed his children from the Riverdale School and has since created a foundation called FAIR, dedicated to confronting the "intolerance and racism" at the heart of identity politics.

Collegiate's response has been to convene a seventeen-member task force to address its "history and symbols." Released after three years of study, the group's 407-page report called for recasting "Peg Leg Pete," the school's Knickerbocker mascot, over its "Eurocentric and racist overtones to its crude depiction of a disability, a peg leg," according to *The New York Times*. More telling, "to make clear that we are a fully inclusive and welcoming community," the report recommended the elimination of the reference to God on the school's seal: *Nisi Dominus Frustra*, "Without the Lord, [it is] in Vain," from Psalm 127. The report concluded:

> In the early years of the school, one of the major areas of focus was proselytizing Native Americans and others to Christianity. There is also a history of Christian hegemony in the United States that has been experienced as both exclusive and oppressive.

Other elite schools have similarly closed progressive ranks. At New York's Dalton School, some parents questioned that institution's anti-racist pledge to abolish any advanced course where black students did not perform as well as their white counterparts. At the annual meeting of diversity heads at the school, the keynote speaker then denounced this parent action for its "plantation mentality" and likened these "white supremacists" to the capitol rioters of January 6. Meanwhile at Spence, the school decided to tear out *Les Vues d'Amérique du Nord*, its ninety-year-old wallpaper designed by Zuber et Cie and only recently restored. The reason? Its "romanticized view," which included both black and white Americans enjoying the countryside together, was "historically inaccurate." In other words, the same wallpaper that was installed in the Kennedy White House in 1961, and which featured prominently in the background of the Obama administration, was removed because it was not racist enough. Meanwhile, the construction of Spence's new multimillion-dollar athletic facility, featuring nine squash courts and an ecology center, went ahead as planned, destroying what remained of St. Joseph's Orphan Asylum.

The well-trained elite

Even as much of America has now rejected the doctrine of Critical Race Theory, due to its exposure by Christopher Rufo and others, elite schools have instituted mandatory "anti-racism" training not just for students and teachers but also for parents, writing these obligations into enrollment and employment contracts. Would Glenn Loury and John McWhorter, outspoken black critics of anti-racism, now even be permitted to send children to such elite schools, let alone be invited to speak? McWhorter, author of *Woke Racism*, has called anti-racism "an illiberal neo-racism" that has "betrayed black America." How about Ayaan Hirsi Ali? The Somali-born activist has written that "Anti-racism is the disease that it purports to cure. Its narratives of resentment are dividing us once again by race, weakening our hard-earned freedom and mutual trust, and threatening our children's future. We have no option but to fight it as we once fought white supremacy." Would such words violate an enrollment contract that is pledged to anti-racism? The answer is that, for all of their independence, the nation's private schools still answer not only to their elite boards but also to accrediting consortia that function as centralized bureaucracies for the diversity industry – groups that have shown little interest in the values of free discourse, equal treatment, rigorous inquiry, or open dissent.

And besides, why should most of today's elites even want to complain? Diversity functions as a prime mechanism of class distraction. To elite sensitivities, "Black Lives Matter" sounds better than "Occupy Wall Street" – even as both movements have emerged from the illiberal Left. Racial activists and corporate America have developed a robust working relationship that promotes each of their interests. The elites get a hustle; the activists make a profit. Writing in *Liberties Journal*, the literary scholar William Deresiewicz, who has been critical of the "excellent sheep" raised in the folds of elite education, locates the assimilation of minority elites into this progressive culture:

> It is elites within the Hispanic community who say "Latinx"; the vast majority of Latinos hate the word, when they have even heard of it. It is elites within the black community who propagate the dogma of critical race theory; blacks on average are actually more moderate than the typical white Democrat. It is elites within the Asian-American community who inveigh against assimilation;

most Asian-Americans are busily assimilating. But then so are the elites, of all groups – so especially are the elites – and it is only their bad conscience, or, more charitably, their understandable ambivalence, that leads them to imagine otherwise.

Elites of many stripes have learned to benefit from the culture of identity politics. The prerogatives of black activism are now claimed by their white "allies." A spectrum of grievances can shift from race to gender to other protected classes until it encompasses the elites' own. The end result is that, from the British royal family on down, we are now presented with an aristocracy of grievance. The higher up we go, the greater the affront. After witnessing the shock of trans activists pushing their way into women's sports, for example, we might soon see a generation of nonbinary athletes angling for their own division in college sports – and a legion of elite coaches, trainers, and professionals to make sure they get there. Unlike the shady dealings of "Varsity Blues," however, an elite student shuttled through the pipeline to the nonbinary wing of the Princeton fencing program would be heralded in news stories – "a first!" – while dissenters would be branded as transphobes or TERFs, for "trans-exclusionary radical feminists."

Diversity can indeed be "trained." For the well-mannered elite, it is an easy game to play. Regulations always benefit insiders. The "diversity lens" offers up polarizing glasses that leave the world simplified into black and white and easier for their charges to master. The new, anything-goes rules of human gender are easier to learn than the old nuances of French gender. It is easier to fixate on human races than Latin cases – despite the talk of "Latinx."

It is also easier to discount the plight of America's underclass when you cannot see it. Those who disagree are denounced as racist and "deplorable."

Such provincials, of course, make up the vast majority of Americans, both black and white. They reject elite dogma. So their class complaints are redirected into race complaints. Or for their faith in America, they are written off for false consciousness. Or their protests over workplace restrictions are "unanimously condemned" for somehow promoting "anti-Semitism, Islamophobia, anti-Black racism, homophobia, and transphobia," as the Canadian Prime Minister Justin Trudeau said of his country's trucker revolt. "Together, let's keep working to make Canada more inclusive," he concluded. How much better – so our elites would maintain – for power to be handed over to them. Only they have been trained in the language of identity. Only they have been conditioned in the syntax of grievance. Only they have worked their whole lives so as not to misgender others. The elites, simply put, will take it from here.

Awaking from the fever dream

As the world again commands our attention, we risk the loss of our own democratic future. This is especially true for a hardworking, non-elite generation that still believes in the blessings of liberty and the universal power of liberal education. Deserving first-generation Asian applicants continue to be kept out of Ivy League schools through an elite system of racial quotas. Meanwhile Dan-el Padilla Peralta – the elite-trained classics professor (Collegiate, Princeton, Oxford, Stanford) who obsesses over the "production of whiteness" residing "in the very marrows of classics" – is fast-tracked for Ivy League tenure.

Yet there is hope, especially from outside progressive circles. Thomas Chatterton Williams, the author of *Self-Portrait in Black and White: Unlearning Race,* writes about the transformation experienced by his black father in segregated Texas upon discovering Plato's dialogues. Roosevelt Montás, an immigrant from the Dominican Republic and the author of *Rescuing Socrates: How the Great Books Changed My Life and Why They Matter for a New Generation,* had a similar encounter with the classics and now passes on that knowledge: "My students from low-income households do not take this sort of thinking to be the exclusive privilege of a social elite. In fact they find in it a vision of dignity and excellence that is not constrained by material limitations."

Over half a century ago, believing that the salvation of our culture could be effected by its elite class, William F. Buckley Jr. proposed writing a book called *The Revolt Against the Masses* as his own answer to José Ortega y Gasset. Witnessing the elite self-abnegation of the 1960s, he was never able to finish it. Concerned citizens must now shake elite culture from its fever dream. Free-speech leftists, cultural conservatives, Great Books liberals, traditional feminists – all must realize the role they play in this awakening. The time is right for a revolt *for* the masses. But for any true reckoning, today's elites must also look to themselves and their own decadent isolation. At the crossroads of Western civilization, the signs point to our democratic salvation or our common ruin.

Culture against Civilization

JAMES PIERESON

THE DISTINGUISHED TRADITION of art, literature, and philosophy that has defined the Western world for more than two millennia is collapsing almost everywhere. It has been abandoned in the colleges, reinterpreted according to contemporary conventions, attacked in the name of multiculturalism, and rejected all around as a "white man's" enterprise. It is impossible to defend it without being dismissed in ruling circles as a reactionary or an old fogey enamored with the past. Students who a generation or two ago might have taken courses in Western civilization or studied Plato and Aristotle, or Michelangelo and Raphael, or Locke and the *Federalist* papers are now lectured by their teachers about race, gender, and sexuality. They know little of Greek philosophy, the history of Rome, the origins of the great religions, the architecture of medieval churches, or the development of Enlightenment ideas that created the modern world. They seem to know just as little about the history of the United States or how well off they are compared to earlier generations.

The interest groups and ideological factions that have taken over the contemporary university view the Western tradition as an obstacle to reform or revolution. "Hey hey, ho ho, Western Civ has got to go," cried radical students and faculty at one campus a few decades ago. Other students, not quite so politicized, nevertheless view "Western Civ" as useless or irrelevant to their vocational interests and so lack the tools by which they might challenge their teachers. In any case, the radicals achieved their aim. No one yet knows what will happen as those students take their one-sided ideas or lack of knowledge from the academy into the wider world of business, government, publishing, and teaching. Thus far, the signs are not encouraging.

At the same time, Western institutions seem as strong and influential as ever, both at home and abroad. People around the world still try to emulate American and European patterns of government, business, science, and law, though mostly without success. That is why so many continue to stream across borders into Europe and the United States. Americans have not yet lost faith in the Constitution, popular government, the rule of law, and progress through free markets and scientific knowledge. Those in and around the universities who attack Western civilization do so because they resent its achievements and success or find it wanting when viewed in light of its own high ideals. They both hate and admire the West at the same time. Few seem inclined to pick up and leave in order to live under other civilizational ideals or conditions. Their goal, rather, is to take over – but to what end?

If civilization is defined in terms of stable governments and the rule of law, trusted currencies, leading universities and research institutions, productive business corporations, and widely admired ideals, then Western civilization appears to be as strong or even stronger now than it was a century or seventy-five years ago when it was recovering from catastrophic wars and had not yet spread around the globe. Far from receding, the civilization of the West has evolved into a worldwide enterprise.

Is the West collapsing, or is it thriving? On the evidence, it can be hard to tell. The correct answer might be some of both. In the arena of culture, the inheritance of the West is in decline; in regard to the institutions of civilization, it still advances. The meaning of this, and how it has happened, are questions that do not admit of easy answers. Will the attack on Western ideas and ideals lead to a collapse of the civilizational institutions that arose from them? Or might the continuing strength of those institutions provoke a revival of those ideas?

A tale of two half centuries

The achievements of Western Civilization over the second half of the twentieth century were as impressive as was the scale of destruction inflicted upon it in the wars of the first half of the century. Between eighty and one hundred million people were killed in the world wars of 1914–18 and 1939–45, numbers that must be augmented by casualties, refugees, and the victims of murder and genocide, and mass starvation, all of which cannot account for the ruin of churches, libraries, and museums that had taken centuries to build. Not since the fall of Rome had the West encountered a time of crisis comparable to the bloody crossroads of the 1900–50 period. The catastrophe was magnified by the progress of the previous era as new technologies created to produce wealth were redirected toward purposes of war. Those wars might have destroyed civilization for centuries if liberal Europe had not been backed up by a sister civilization in the United States that aided mightily in its victory and recovery.

In contrast to Europe (and Japan), the United States emerged intact from the wars as the world's wealthiest and most powerful nation, with losses of life and treasure on a minor scale compared to those suffered elsewhere. The sense of relief and good fortune felt by Americans in the middle of the century was tempered by the reality of the Cold War and the threat posed by communism to their freedom and prosperity. But two decades of war and depression had a way of dampening expectations for the future. If there were fears for the future of civilization, then they arose from the risks of nuclear war, communism and tyranny, or another economic collapse, certainly not from thoughts of cultural dissolution.

In the middle of the century, George Orwell set forth the grim vision of what was likely to happen in the post-war decades in his dystopian novel *Nineteen Eighty-Four*, published in 1949, in which he looked ahead to a world divided into totalitarian superstates: Oceania versus Eurasia versus East Asia. These powers exist in a condition of perpetual warfare even though there are no principled differences among them. It is useful to keep the masses ("proles") in a state of martial anxiety as a means of controlling them. Great Britain, known as Airstrip One, is a piece of Oceania, which is, along with the Americas, governed by "Big Brother," who prescribes and enforces morally approved views: "Peace is Strength," "War is Peace," and so on. The English language disappears into "Newspeak." The "Thought Police" root out disapproved ideas. Old people cannot be trusted: "Those whose ideas were formed before the Revolution cannot have a full understanding of English socialism." Winston and Julia, at first loyal party members, rebel in defense of their individuality but cannot succeed against the totalitarian forces arrayed against them. At length, after a round of torture and reeducation, Winston discovers again his loyalty to Big Brother.

The novel suggested that communism would eventually overwhelm the West and impose a soul-destroying dictatorship, but, in fairness, Orwell wrote *Nineteen Eighty-Four* as a cautionary tale showing what might happen rather than a prediction of what would happen. Still, it was not a farfetched possibility, because there were many who shared those fears. Whittaker Chambers, for example, wrote in *Witness* (1952) that communism would eventually prevail because it was a fighting faith while the West was losing belief in itself.

The Harvard economist Sumner H. Schlichter expressed the opposite view in a series of articles and speeches in 1949 and 1950. Looking decades into the future (like Orwell), he wrote that the United States was about to experience an unprecedented revolution of rising living standards and with it would arise a greater appreciation of the capitalist system. By 1980, he said, the U.S. population would grow to 175 million (from 150 million in 1950), the workforce would expand to seventy-two million (from sixty-two million), labor productivity would double to 4 percent per year, the output of goods and services would double, and the economy would grow in excess of 3 percent per year. He predicted that the United States would become a country of two-car families by 1980 with seventy million automobiles on the road. The proportion of young people graduating from high school and college would increase; medical services would improve and would be widely used; air-conditioning would be universal and home swimming pools popular. He thought that the work week might be cut to thirty hours and that "the arts will flourish as never before in the history of the world." Schlichter's forecasts were widely dismissed as too optimistic in view of recent decades of depression and war and the new reality of the Cold War.

In the event, it was the Harvard economist's views that eventually proved true as the United States soon enjoyed a revolution in rising living standards that few had anticipated in 1950. In fact, Schlichter's rosy forecasts fell far short of the mark. The U.S. population grew to 225 million by 1980, doubling in three decades and far surpassing expectations, and to 281 million by the year 2000. The labor force expanded to 107 million in 1980 and to 144 million by the end of the century. Labor productivity doubled, as he predicted, while the output of goods and services tripled between 1950 and 1980 as the U.S. economy grew in excess of 4 percent per year during the 1950s and 1960s. The percentage of the population with high-school diplomas increased from 34 to 67 percent, and the number of students attending colleges increased by five or six times over those three decades. By 1980 there were 122 million automobiles on the road, just about two per household, swimming pools were common, and air-conditioning was nearly universal. Contra Orwell, international communism collapsed during the 1980s, not long after the dread year of 1984, in part because of pressure from the West, but also because it could not be made to work. The economist Schlichter was wrong about one thing: for the most part the arts did not flourish in the post-war era, even as more money flowed into them.

It would be easy to document in further detail the achievements of Western civilization, led by the United States, in those post-war decades from 1950 to 2000. The United States underwrote the recovery of Western Europe with loans and credits, brought those countries (along with Japan) into a new trading system, and held the line against communism until that system collapsed. Life expectancy increased from sixty years in 1950 to close to eighty years in 2000, aided by advances in medicine and wealth; death rates from heart disease and cancer fell, food prices declined in relation to incomes, indoor plumbing and electricity were made universally available (television as well), and improved products and leisure were placed within the reach of millions who did not dream of them in 1950. Opportunities for advancement were extended to women and racial minorities. The taming of inflation and the explosion of the stock markets after 1980 created still more wealth and many millionaires and billionaires, while underwriting new companies and impressive technologies that similarly elevated living standards over the next several decades. Even China, insanely revolutionary as recently as the 1970s, scrapped communism as an economic policy (though not as a political doctrine). Since 1990, in great part due to Western policies, more than 1.2 billion people around the world have risen out of extreme poverty; today less than 10 percent of the world's population lives in poverty, compared to 36 percent in 1990.

These figures scratch the surface as measures of worldwide progress that the West promoted and achieved across the postwar decades. It was a record of civilizational progress that has no parallel in the history of the world, and which stands in extraordinary contrast to the events of 1900 to 1945.

Adversaries of culture

In 2020, near the beginning of the coronavirus pandemic, agitators stormed into the streets of large cities across the country in protest against the death of a black man while in police custody in Minneapolis. They remained in the streets all summer, far longer than necessary to make their point, in New York, Portland, Seattle, Los Angeles, and (of course) Minneapolis, smashing windows, burning businesses, surrounding federal buildings, attacking the police, even burning and looting police headquarters in one city, under the guise of protest against racism, police brutality, and inequality. Leading politicians, all Democrats, joined the protests, though many of those officials continued to enforce restrictions on large gatherings due to the coronavirus pandemic. (It was said to be permissible to attend gatherings for "just" causes.) Democrats approved of the protests, along with the accompanying violence, because they understood them to be helpful for the presidential election in the fall. In short order, nearly every university in the country issued statements in support of the protests and in denunciation of the police, and so also did many corporations and every professional sports league. Even formerly sober and stuffy Brooks Brothers issued a statement of support, while protestors smashed windows near its longtime flagship store on Madison Avenue in New York City. It seemed that half the country, and leaders of every major institution, supported the mobs, even as they targeted the police, small businesses, property owners, and the middle-class rules of conduct.

The eruptions should not have come as a surprise. Similar protests, though not quite on this scale, had been staged countless times in the years leading up to the events of 2020. In addition, the movements behind the protests had been building up momentum and support across the board for decades going back to the 1960s. The wealth accumulated in the post-war era established the foundations for a formidable adversary culture in the cities and around the universities in tension with the institutions of the wider society. In time, this culture took over the universities and infiltrated government, charitable organizations, journalism, and even major corporations. That was one reason those courses in Western civilization disappeared from college curricula. It happened that the "soldiers" of this culture took to the streets in 2020, but with the express support of the leaders and shapers at the top of America's institutional pyramid.

Several insightful thinkers, Lionel Trilling, Irving Kristol, and Roger Kimball high on that list, have written that American culture evolved during the post-war era in a manner critical of, often hostile to, the market economy and bourgeois civilization responsible for so much progress after 1950. Trilling pointed to an "adversary culture" of intellectuals, mainly college professors and writers, who could not help but adopt a critical posture toward the civilization that supported them. He thought that this critical disposition kept them from seeing the society as it actually is but doubted that they could ever become numerous or influential enough to take over. Kristol took the idea a step further in viewing the adversary culture in terms of a "new class" of educators, journalists, and bureaucrats that developed a common interest that went beyond expanding their numbers or taking over institutions within their reach, such as colleges or magazines. He wrote that the new class has a more profound interest in challenging the institutions of bourgeois society, including corporations, the free market, and the nuclear family, and in promoting ideas at odds with middle-class notions of individualism and individual responsibility, self-discipline, and marriage.

Members of the new class, he wrote, gravitated to academe and government, where they consolidated and expanded their influence. They liked to make rules for others to follow and to make up new ones at their convenience. They claimed to speak for the poor, later for women and minorities, eventually for the downtrodden everywhere. Their moral posture was one source of influence, in contrast to the self-interested conduct of everyone else. This gave them latitude to break rules others were obliged to follow. As Kristol wrote decades ago,

> The problem today is located in the culture of our society which is in the process of outflanking our relatively successful economy. While the society is bourgeois, the culture is increasingly and belligerently not.

These terms, while still applicable, require some modification. The adversary culture is no longer composed of alienated intellectuals and writers but instead consists of a large class of bureaucrats, administrators, activists, academic hangers-on and would-be theorists, and wealthy patrons. It is larger, more varied, and vastly more influential that it was in Trilling's day. The "new class," as Kristol suggests, is of post-war origin and finds its identity in opposition to middle-class institutions and ideals. It is a good question whether the "new class" should be understood principally by its interests like other classes in society, as Kristol suggested, or whether it is more a movement with broad ideological goals and an ambition to take control of government. It has features that set it apart from established interest groups. Its members disdain negotiation and compromise, much like ideological groups in other times and places. Their goals are comprehensive and not easy to satisfy: ending racism and sexism; eliminating the police; saving the planet. Every concession seems to provoke new demands. They see their adversaries as unsophisticated or untutored, more frequently racist and sexist. For these reasons, they do not coexist comfortably with other groups in society.

This "new class" or "adversary culture," whatever one wishes to call it, has turned out to be far more influential than any left-wing movement of the past, in large part because it is composed of middle- and upper-class professionals, rather than the outsiders or proletarians of Marxist theory. They are well placed by those positions to leverage reformist or radical ideas, communicate them to others, or force them upon unwary or disorganized citizens. The radicals of the 1960s eventually rejected the revolutionary strategy in favor of the "long march" through the institutions, as Roger Kimball has described. That was made possible by the post-war boom that provided wealth for the expansion of colleges, charitable groups, public-employee unions, and the federal government, while also financing the welfare state that the new class administers and seeks to expand. While in the 1960s the same people might have been isolated on the campus or in fringe newspapers and magazines, they now seem to be everywhere: in government, sometimes directing government agencies, writing for *The New York Times*, teaching in Ivy League institutions, running corporations and Wall Street investment houses, and campaigning for national office. The "new class" has exploded in numbers and influence and is in the process of taking over the main institutions of bourgeois civilization. Though it has been called a "culture," it looks now more like an alternative civilization threatening to take control of the country – if, in fact, it has not already done so.

It comes armed with a theory, or more precisely an ideology, revolving around identity, in this case the identities of race, gender, and sexuality (further identities may be added). Having originated as a means of extending opportunity to new groups, the culture devolved, perhaps by design, into an inflexible doctrine known as "diversity." The central ideas are that these groups have been oppressed in the past by American society, that they deserve recognition and compensation as a result, and that it is now their turn to get even with those responsible for their suffering. It is, as many have pointed out, a bastardized version of Marxism in which the working class is expelled as the locus of suffering and exploitation and replaced by race and gender groups defined by "identity."

Here is a poisonous doctrine and also a formula for conflict and civilizational decline. It was cranked out in the universities decades ago and at length has spread everywhere as a bill of grievances against America. Functioning like an ideology in the Marxist sense, it is a body of ideas designed for warfare against enemies. This is one factor that gives its adherents the look of a movement or crusade instead of an interest group. Advocates do not hold their ideas on a tentative basis, for example, as a body of thought subject to revision, but rather as a total doctrine attached to the identities of its bearers. That is true much more of the leaders and activists than of its voters and followers. Any member who thinks about holding the doctrine up for analysis or evaluation is already on his or her way out of the community. Former communists have testified to this cast of mind in great detail, and, like communists, the theorists of diversity are always on the lookout for departures from correct doctrine. Because of this, even tame criticisms of the doctrine are understood by insiders as attacks on their identities – as personal attacks on them or general attacks on the identity groups. It seems impossible to criticize them or adopt different views without making them angry or hurting their feelings. Well-meaning attempts to hold debates about identity politics are thus met with cries of racism, sexism, or homophobia. The crusading mentality has allowed them to take over entire institutions on the grounds that opponents or those who do not share their views are mortal enemies. The advocates of identity are aggressive in pushing their doctrines in whatever bureaucratic or academic settings they find themselves but at the same time extremely sensitive to criticisms from those unwilling to go along or untutored about the nature of the debates taking place.

Members of this class have taken up residence in government and the universities, also in the cities, and are now mostly attached to the Democratic Party, which they are remaking by expelling traditional working-class members and replacing them with voters and cadres of their own type. In this exchange, Democratic officials may have sacrificed many ordinary voters for more elite voters with influence and a coalition of the past for an alliance of the future. The Democrats have abandoned the old-time platform of economic growth and opportunity in favor of the diversity ideology, which is now the operating doctrine of the Democratic Party, much as "New Deal liberalism" had filled that role from the 1930s through the 1960s.

Democrats are far along in the process of building a coalition of the "top and bottom" against the middle: on the one side there are the members of the new class in combination with various client groups that can claim to be victims of middle-class society; on the other, we find those middle-class institutions and voters, along with their principles, ideals, and way of life. The list of victim groups has expanded over the years, much to the advantage of this coalition and those who orchestrate it. As these groups moved into the Democratic Party, others exited to join with Republicans, setting up a struggle between the parties that mirrors the clash of cultures – or, indeed, a clash of civilizations that by definition will be difficult to negotiate.

It is anyone's guess how this conflict will be fought out or how it will be resolved – if, in fact, it can be resolved. There will be no secession or civil war of the kind that happened in 1860, as some think likely. This is not principally a sectional struggle, nor is it likely that factions will take up arms against one another – not yet, anyway. The competition will be fought out in other ways. Every election will be viewed as a contest over the future of the country, with everything staked on the outcome. Under those circumstances, it will be difficult to bind participants to traditional rules according to which elections are fought over limited issues and everyone comes together afterwards to move forward. Contestants will use new stratagems and tactics to suppress speech, harass opponents, bend election rules, and make sure government cannot work whenever opponents get control of it. The different sides will use the powers of government to weaken the opposition or disqualify candidates, perhaps at some point to arrest them or throw them in jail. In this the Left is far ahead of conservatives in its willingness to suspend traditional doctrines in order to wield power. Nevertheless, those lines, once crossed, will not be heeded again and similar measures will be reciprocated by the other side. There will be no serious efforts toward bipartisan compromise; that approach cannot be squared with the totalizing nature of current conflicts.

It is hard to imagine how the United States will be able to function either internationally or domestically in a situation in which the parties are so fervently at odds and represent different civilizational ideas.

James Piereson

A grim picture

This may be taken as an extreme or excessively dire rendering of the current situation, but many troubling developments along these lines have already come to pass: the financial crisis of 2008, with the failure of households, the bailout of banks and accompanying public debt, and a slow recovery; the disastrous military ventures in Iraq and Afghanistan; the politicization of the IRS and FBI in the Obama years; the populist rise of Donald Trump; the contested election of 2016, with out-in-the-open proposals to nullify the election; the Russia "hoax" orchestrated by the press and the FBI, along with efforts to impeach the president; the Kavanaugh hearings; protests in the streets in 2020, inflamed further by the coronavirus pandemic; assassinations of police officers around the country; another contested election in 2020; charges and countercharges from both parties about rigging election rules; protests and riots at the Capitol on January 6, 2021; efforts by Democrats to end the filibuster in the Senate in order to "pack" the Supreme Court – the list goes on. By the looks of things, the contest is just getting started. Meanwhile, China and Russia are watching with great interest, wondering how they might exploit the unraveling situation in the United States. Russia has already made one aggressive move with the invasion of neighboring Ukraine.

There is another way in which this description is not so dire as it might be – because it lays current and future troubles at the doorstep of political and cultural conflicts, while assuming the American economy expands, government is not overwhelmed with debt, the U.S. dollar continues to serve as the reserve currency for the world, prices remain stable, and the stock market continues along on its four-decade boom. It would be unwise to take any or all of these for granted in looking to the American future. A setback in any of these areas will aggravate mightily the tensions and conflicts described above, all of which are serious enough already. Such signs may already be on the horizon. Inflation is running, at the time of this writing, at 8 percent per year, higher than at any time since 1982. That will drive up interest rates and cause trouble for the stock market, which will make it harder for government to service its debt or add new debt, while limiting the capacity of policy-makers to increase spending as a means of papering over political conflicts across society.

Nor are there good reasons to think the U.S. economy will expand in the twenty-first century as it did in those post-war decades between 1950 and 2000. Post-war economic growth peaked in the United States in the 1950s and 1960s, with average real increases of more than 4 percent per year, then slowed to 3 percent per year in the three decades between 1970 and 2000, and then fell rapidly to just 2 percent per year in the two decades from 2000 to 2020. The financial crisis of 2008 inflicted more damage upon the economy than any event since 1950, leading to ever more government while upending consumer and investor confidence for many years thereafter. Americans have taken on debt to substitute for the proceeds of growth: the national debt of the United States now exceeds $30 trillion, with the government borrowing more than $2 trillion annually in recent years (or 10 percent of gross domestic product) to finance its budget. This level of borrowing might have been forestalled if the economy had expanded in recent decades at 3 or 4 percent instead of 2 percent per year. If that had been the case, then U.S. GDP would this year be between $30 and $40 trillion, instead of $23 trillion. But the debt is there, requiring robust economic growth to generate resources just to pay the interest.

The economist Robert Gordon, reversing the confidence of Professor Schlichter in 1950, now argues that the robust economic growth Americans enjoyed during much of the twentieth century was a singular event driven by a series of innovations unlikely to be repeated. The computer and the internet, along with their many contemporary applications, will not come close to matching the prosperity created in the last century by the development of electricity, the internal-combustion engine, indoor plumbing, and modern communications. In Gordon's view, and he marshals much information in support of it, the golden age of American prosperity ended near the close of the last century. He did not examine the extent to which the frictional effects of the adversary culture might have further slowed down economic growth by undermining the work ethic, castigating business enterprise, tolerating crime and social dissolution, and promoting government debt and regulation – as Joseph Schumpeter had forecast in *Capitalism, Socialism, and Democracy* (1942). In any case, as Gordon and others suggest, Americans, much like the Japanese in recent years, may have to accommodate themselves to the new reality of slowing growth and slowly improving living standards. That is a sobering warning for a country accustomed to rapid growth that is also deeply in debt and already dealing with profound cultural and civilizational divisions.

Where it's going

The view from the year 2000 was more confident and hopeful, and probably more complacent, than it was in 1950. The future seemed laid out more clearly in 2000 than in 1950. The Cold War was gone and with it threats of communism, dictatorship, and nuclear war. Fears from abroad were linked to terrorism, not traditional war, while concerns about climate change replaced the economic anxieties of 1950. Economic growth and continued prosperity were more or less taken for granted after fifty years of rising living standards.

When in 1999 the editors of *Time* magazine listed the great accomplishments of the previous half century, they emphasized the expansion of democracy, the defeat of totalitarianism, the steady advance of civil rights, and breakthroughs in technology culminating in the everyday use of computers. They did not mention the post-war boom. Albert Einstein was *Time*'s "Man of the Century," with Franklin Delano Roosevelt and Gandhi following in second and third place. Winston Churchill, *Time*'s "Man of the Half Century" in 1950, was not listed, no doubt because the editors decided that his civilizational achievements were neutralized by other aspects of his career, such as his efforts to maintain the British Empire. The editors, like most everyone else, thought that the early decades of the new century would bring continued progress along the lines that Americans had enjoyed over the previous half century.

That outlook proved to be excessively optimistic, in view of events of the first two decades of the century, just as the outlook in 1950 proved to be too uncertain and pessimistic in light of later developments. Few predicted two or three decades ago that the diversity ideology would gain its current stranglehold over schools, colleges, government, and the Democratic Party – yet that is what has happened. It represents a repudiation of Western ideals and much that the United States has stood for in terms of individual liberty, limited government, strong families, robust civic institutions, and the like. There is little point any longer in pretending that this is not happening.

This raises the real possibility that the civilizational conflicts now in play in the United States will gradually turn it into something resembling a third world country, with a stagnant or declining economy, periodic debt and currency crises, schools and colleges organized around ideology rather than learning, entrenched interests arrogating power and wealth to themselves, other citizens exiting for opportunities elsewhere, and dynamic groups and regions looking for routes of escape from a crumbling system. Something resembling this process is already beginning to unfold across the United States as more and more Americans abandon blue states in favor of red ones and leave the large cities for suburbs and small towns, sometimes in search of better opportunities but often looking for refuge from diversity fanatics in charge of their towns, schools, and states. Sadly, there are already areas in the United States where residents endure conditions similar to those in third world countries. It would not take much to push the United States further in that direction. That is a grim prospect – the "third worldization" of the United States – but not one to be discounted out of hand.

Yet it is also true that events can turn quickly, in any and all directions, notwithstanding expert predictions and logical suppositions based on contemporary conditions. That is why gloomy forecasts do not often work out in America: the American people find ways to refute them. It could happen again. An economic bust might force the country to put its financial house in order after an orgy of spending and borrowing made possible by fifty years of good times. The same is true of a foreign crisis: with their backs to the wall, Americans may demonstrate the resolve of former times. In times of real stress, the cultural issues that have divided the country may turn out to be expendable. In that case, the United States might lead a revival of Western ideals and institutions, much as it did in the post-war era. But a shock of some kind may be required to provoke such a turnaround.

Someone once remarked that in the United States there has always been a race between dynamism and decadence – with dynamism always running a few steps ahead. Yet all signs suggest that decadence – today expressed mostly in the diversity ideology – is catching up, bringing America and the West closer to a new "crossroads of civilization."

Highways to Utopia

ROGER KIMBALL

Every "Age of Enlightenment" proceeds from an
unlimited optimism of the reason ... to an equally
unqualified skepticism.

OSWALD SPENGLER
The Decline of the West

Day by day, month by month, doubt by doubt, law and order
became fascism; education, constraint; work, alienation;
revolution, mere sport; leisure, a privilege of class;
marijuana, a harmless weed; family, a stifling hothouse;
affluence, oppression; success, a social disease; sex, an
innocent pastime; youth, a permanent tribunal; maturity,
the new senility; discipline, an attack on personality;
Christianity ... and the West ... and white skin.

JEAN RASPAIL
The Camp of the Saints

A T LEAST SINCE Oedipus met King Laius at the narrow fork
where the road from Delphi to Thebes split off to Daulis, the
image of a crossroads has signaled a dramatic and morally fraught
turning point. A lot of ink has been spilt pondering the question
whether the turn is something fated or the result of a choice.

Robert Frost, in his famous poem, took "the road less traveled," and it "made all the difference." Could Oedipus have done likewise? Or did Sophocles load the dice against poor Oedipus? Aristotle, in his commentary on the plays, says that Oedipus's fate was the result of a flaw for which he bore the guilt, though not, exactly, the responsibility.

That is the way things go with the apparently inexorable dialectic of hubris, infatuation, and nemesis (yielding in the end to catharsis and resolution, not that it did Oedipus much good).

Contrasting the "indulgence" shown by liberal intellectuals towards the gritty realist Theodore Dreiser and the severity shown by them to Henry James, the literary critic Lionel Trilling spoke of "the dark and bloody crossroads where literature and politics meet." In "our world of impending disaster," Trilling said, confronting that crossroads was unavoidable for anyone attending to "reality in America," though he remained somewhat elliptical about the burdens of the different courses being mapped. What Trilling calls "the ultimate question" – "of what use, of what actual political use" are James's novels? – is a puzzle that might baffle Oedipus. Still, Trilling's memorable formulation has a significance that transcends his discussion of Dreiser and James. His "dark and bloody crossroads" also stands before us, posing different and perhaps even more ultimate questions.

One of the more beneficent and also enigmatic early Greek goddesses is Hecate, the only daughter of the titans Perses and Asteria. Among other things, the three-faced goddess stands as a talisman at crossroads, junctions whose alternative routes may mark not only alternative destinations but also alternative destinies. "*Ora vides Hecates in tres vertentia partes,*" Ovid writes in his poem on the Roman calendar of festivals, "*servet ut in ternas compita secta vias*": "See Hecate's faces turned in three directions that she may guard the branching crossroads."

Ovid's description is upbeat. But for some time past, the mood in the West, among intellectuals, anyway, has listed towards the gloomy. Hecate, if she is on hand at all, seems to glower more than guard. In the 1940s, Cyril Connolly sighed that it was "closing time in the gardens of the West." A couple of decades before that, in the immediate aftermath of the shambles that was World War I, Oswald Spengler gave definitive expression to the temperament of the times in his sprawling Teutonic threnody *Der Untergang des Abendlandes*, "The Decline of the West."

At some point the West really will decline. Is it finally happening? And what is this "West" that is "declining," "closing," facing a momentous crossroads? An incomplete but not inaccurate shorthand is "Christendom." I know that the term strikes an antique note in America *circa* 2022. When is the last time you heard someone utter it without invisible scare quotes? (When was the last time you heard someone utter it at all?) But a decaying moral vocabulary – consider the recent career of words like "virtue," "manliness," "womanly," or "respectable" – is part of the ominous cargo we are called upon to bear. As for "Christendom," it names a dispensation in which the individual possesses intrinsic moral worth, defined not only by the Christian tradition itself but buoyed also by those traditions, predominantly classical and Judaic, which flowed into and helped nurture and define that baggy creation we call "the West."

One bleak route on the crossroads we face involves the willful throttling of those mighty currents. Angry at the Gyndes River for sweeping away and drowning one of his sacred white horses, Cyrus decided to punish the river by having his slaves cut

360 channels into it, stanching its flow to a trickle. This we have done to ourselves, applying mental tourniquets to the arteries that fed us from the past in order that we might gambol undisturbed in distracted present-tense ignorance. An illustrative case in point is the Princeton classics department, where woke educationists panting for relevance recently jettisoned the requirement that its students learn Latin or Greek, never mind both. At the same time, they publicly celebrate the fifty-seven varieties of racial-trans-wonderfulness that have become the focus of academic obsession. It is a situation that is as absurd as it is malignant. In *The Present Age* (1846), Kierkegaard described the jaded spirit that "leaves everything standing but cunningly empties it of significance." That is where we are today: occupying a husk of decadence assiduously emptied of vitality. Princeton, Yale, Harvard, and the rest of the querulous educational establishment are sodden with money but spiritually and intellectually bankrupt. They continue to *look like* educational institutions: leafy walks, imposing libraries, impressive buildings. But most of the activities they sponsor are inimical to real education, inciting thousands of puny Cyruses to divert and stymie the waters of tradition in order to polish the mirror of their narcissism.

Dynamism & deviancy

It is often said that a distinguishing feature of Western civilization is its "dynamism," its tendency to change, to foment opposition and critical self-reflection. By contrast, ancient Egyptian, Chinese, and other cultures sought longevity through stasis. Among other things, the element of percolation that is part of the West's identity inscribes a certain irony into its DNA. Often, seeds of its perpetuation blossom into more or less fundamental challenges to its legacy. Just so, Marxism and its many allotropes and subsidiaries are deeply anti-Western and at the same time typical products of that peculiar dynamism that defines the West. The ideologies of "wokeness" and identity politics belong here: blunt, untutored manifestations of the "transvaluation of all values" that Nietzsche spoke about in one of his agitated moods. Perhaps this self-canceling aspect of the West is part of what James Hankins and Allen C. Guelzo had in mind when they noted in the first chapter of this volume, "Civilization & Tradition," that "Civilization is always threatened by barbarism, and the greater threat often comes more from within than from without." The political philosopher James Burnham made a similar point when he argued that "Suicide is probably more frequent than murder as the end phase of a civilization." That the pathology may be self-generated is more an admonition than a consolation.

The historian Arnold Toynbee spoke in this context of the "barbarization of the dominant minority." When a society is robust and self-confident, Toynbee suggested, cultural influence travels largely from the elites to the proletariats. The elites furnish social models to be emulated. The proletariats are "softened," Toynbee said, by their imitation of the manners and morals of a dominant elite. But when a society begins to falter, the imitation proceeds largely in the opposite direction: the dominant elite is coarsened by its imitation of proletarian manners. Toynbee spoke in this context of a growing "sense of drift," "truancy," "promiscuity," and general "vulgarization" of manners, morals, and the arts. The elites, instead of holding fast to their own standards, suddenly begin to "go native" and adopt the dress, attitudes, and behavior of the lower classes. Flip on your television, scroll through social media, look at the teens and pre-teens in your middle-class neighborhood. You will see what Toynbee meant by "barbarization of the dominant [or, rather 'once-dominant'] minority." One part of the impulse is summed up in the French phrase *nostalgie de la boue*. But it is not "mud" that is sought so much as repudiation.

The social scientist Charles Murray, writing about Toynbee in *The Wall Street Journal* back in 2001, noted how closely the historian's analysis fit developments in contemporary America. To a large extent, it is a matter of failed or discarded ideals. "Truancy and promiscuity, in Toynbee's sense," Murray writes,

> are not new in America. But until a few decades ago they were publicly despised and largely confined to the bottom layer of Toynbee's proletariat – the group we used to call "low-class" or "trash," and which we now call the underclass. Today, those behaviors have been transmuted into a code that the elites sometimes imitate, sometimes placate, and fear to challenge. Meanwhile, they no longer have a code of their own in which they have confidence.

What we are talking about is the drift, the tendency of our culture. And that is to be measured not so much by what we permit or forbid as by what we unthinkingly accept as normal. This crossroads, that is to say, is part of a process, one of whose markers is the normalization of the outré. Senator Daniel Patrick Moynihan described this development as "defining deviancy down." It is, as the late columnist Charles Krauthammer observed, a two-way process. "As part of the vast social project of moral leveling," he wrote, it is not enough for the deviant to be normalized. The normal must be found to be deviant.... Large areas of ordinary behavior hitherto considered benign have had their threshold radically redefined up, so that once innocent behavior now stands condemned as deviant. Normal middle-class life then stands exposed as the true home of violence and abuse and a whole catalog of aberrant acting and thinking.

Hilaire Belloc espied the culmination of this process in *Survivals and New Arrivals* (1929):

When it is mature we shall have, not the present isolated, self-conscious insults to beauty and right living, but a positive coordination and organized affirmation of the repulsive and the vile.

The sage of Ecclesiastes informs us that "there is nothing new under the sun." But there are many aspects of our culture today that put that claim to the test. Michael Anton, in his contribution to this volume, provides an inventory of developments that, taken together, support his contention that our situation is (as he said in his title) "unprecedented."

In some ways, Anton's list reads like a variation on the litany offered in the passage from Jean Raspail's *Camp of the Saints* (1973) that I quote as an epigraph. That dystopian novel imagines a world in which Western civilization is overrun and destroyed by unfettered third-world immigration. It describes an instance of wholesale cultural suicide in which demography is weaponized and deployed as an instrument of retribution. Conspicuous in that apocalypse is the feckless collusion of white Europeans and Americans in their own supersession. They faced an existential crossroads. They chose extinction, laced with the emotion of higher virtue, rather than survival.

Although published in the early 1970s, *Camp of the Saints* sounds a distinctly contemporary note. Ibram X. Kendi is not actually a character in Raspail's book. But he might have stepped right out of its pages. "The only remedy to racist discrimination," Kendi has written, "is antiracist discrimination. The only remedy to past discrimination is present discrimination. The only remedy to present discrimination is future discrimination." In other words, Kendi advises race-based discrimination today, race-based discrimination tomorrow, race-based discrimination forever. Compare Raspail:

> Now, it's a known fact that racism comes in two forms: that practiced by whites – heinous and inexcusable, whatever its motives – and that practiced by blacks – quite justified, whatever its excesses, since it's merely the expression of a righteous revenge, and it's up to the whites to be patient and understanding.

This racial spoils-system is one giant totem looming over the crossroads we face. Another is the anti-sexual sexual hypertrophy that has become such a curious feature of our cultural landscape. Back in 1994, Irving Kristol wrote an important essay called "Countercultures." In it he noted that "'Sexual liberation' is always near the top of a countercultural agenda – though just what form the liberation takes can and does vary, sometimes quite widely." The costumes and rhetoric change, but the end is always the same: an assault on the defining institutions of our civilization. "Women's liberation," Kristol continues,

> is another consistent feature of all countercultural movements – liberation from husbands, liberation from children, liberation from family. Indeed, the real object of these various sexual heterodoxies is to disestablish the family as the central institution of human society, the citadel of orthodoxy.

In *Eros and Civilization* (1966), the Marxist countercultural guru Herbert Marcuse provided an illustration of Kristol's thesis *avant la lettre*. Railing against "the tyranny of procreative sexuality," Marcuse urged his followers to return to a state of "primary narcissism" and extolled the joys of "polymorphous perversity." Are we there yet? "Be fruitful, and multiply," the Book of Genesis advised. Marcuse sought to enlist a programmatically unfruitful sexuality in his campaign against "capitalism" and the cultural establishment: barrenness as a revolutionary desideratum. Back then the diktat seemed radical but self-contained, another crackpot effusion from the academy. Today, it is a widespread mental health problem, accepted gospel preached by teachers, the media, and legislators across the country. As I write, the National Women's Law Center has just taken to Twitter to declare that "People of all genders need abortions." How many things had to go wrong for someone, presumably female, to issue that bulletin? "All genders," indeed. I recall the observation, attributed to Voltaire, that "Those who can make you believe absurdities can make you commit atrocities."

In "The Catholic Tradition and the Modern State" (1916), the historian Christopher Dawson wrote that "It is not liberty, but power which is the true note of our modern civilization. Man has gained infinitely in his control over Nature, but he has lost control over his own individual life." I think this is true. And there is a political as well as a technical or scientific dimension to the phenomenon Dawson describes.

In the West, what we have witnessed since the so-called "Progressive" movement of the 1910s and 1920s is the rise of a bureaucratic elite that has increasingly absorbed the prerogatives of power from legislative bodies. In the United States, for example, Article I of the Constitution vests all legislative power in Congress. For many decades, however, Americans have been ruled less by laws duly enacted by their representatives in Congress and more by an alphabet soup of regulatory agencies. The members of these bodies are elected by no one; they typically work outside the purview of public scrutiny; and yet their diktats have the force of law. Already in the 1940s, James Burnham was warning about the prospect of a "managerial revolution" that would accomplish by bureaucracy what traditional politics had failed to produce. Succeeding decades have seen the extraordinary growth of this leviathan, the unchecked multiplication of its offices and powers, and the encroaching reach of its tentacles into the interstices of everyday life. We are now, to an extent difficult to calculate, ruled by this "administrative state," the "deep state," the "regulatory state."

The location of sovereignty

When in September 2020 the World Economic Forum at Davos announced its blueprint for a "Great Reset" in the wake of the worldwide panic over COVID, a new crossroads had been uncovered. Never letting a crisis go to waste, the Davos initiative was an extensive menu of progressive, i.e., socialistic imperatives. Here at last was an opportunity to enact a worldwide tax on wealth, a far-reaching (and deeply impoverishing) "green-energy" agenda, rules that would dilute national sovereignty, and various schemes to insinuate politically correct attitudes into the fabric of everyday life. All this was being promulgated for our own good, of course. But it was difficult to overlook the fact that the WEF plan involved nothing less than the absorption of liberty by the extension of bureaucratic power. "Of all tyrannies," C. S. Lewis wrote,

> a tyranny sincerely exercised for the good of its victims may be the most oppressive. It would be better to live under robber barons than under omnipotent moral busybodies. The robber baron's cruelty may sometimes sleep, his cupidity may at some point be satiated; but those who torment us for our own good will torment us without end for they do so with the approval of their own conscience.

The social commentator Joel Kotkin, noting the class element of this process, has recently traced the emergence of a "neo-feudalist" impulse throughout the West. Drawing on the managerial apparatus of the administrative state, this twenty-first-century form of feudalism lacks the regalia of its medieval precursors. But it operates by enacting an equally thoroughgoing agenda of dependency.

The political scientist John Marini may not have coined the term "administrative state," but he has done more than anyone has to plumb its Stygian depths and anatomize its assaults on liberty. Drawing on Marini's work, the Claremont Institute's Glenn Ellmers has recently articulated the essential tension between constitutional government, which is based upon a broadly shared common sense, and its would-be replacement: technocratic government, which is populated by an unaccountable elite, "experts" whose leading characteristic is faith in their own prerogatives. This "permanent government," Ellmers writes, "is a powerful force":

> It has established its own legitimacy apart from its political or constitutional authority, within the ranks of both political parties and the courts. Bureaucratic rule is defended as essential to solving, in a non-partisan way, the problems of modern government and society. But the bureaucracy has become a political faction on behalf of its own interests. Moreover, the party that defends progressivism and elite authority is increasingly open about politicizing the last vestiges of non-partisan government, including the Justice Department and federal law enforcement. As their power has grown, these defenders of administrative government are increasingly unable to understand, let alone tolerate, anyone who fails to recognize the legitimacy of the administrative state.

As I have noted elsewhere, it is important to acknowledge that this progressive project is as much a Republican as a Democratic pursuit. Despite some rhetorical differences, both parties are fully paid-up worker bees in this hive. The "pragmatic" cover they give themselves is the supposed "complexity" of modern life and complication of contemporary governance. Who but they are equipped to manage the machinery of the state, the minutiae of government? Ellmers nails it: "The pursuit of progress, social justice, and equity becomes for them the moral equivalent of constitutional authority." Welcome to Davos.

Challenging the hegemony of experts requires a widespread reassertion of that "common-sense morality" to which the Founders appealed but which is regarded by our would-be masters as an impediment to utopia. A key problem, as Ellmers sees, is that

> what is left of public morality is now understood in terms of "values," or subjective preferences based only on individual will. Even in the small handful of healthy institutions in civil society, the political and civil rights of the ordinary citizen rest upon a precarious foundation, threatened and undermined by the powerful claims of social progress.

Those claims are nearly irrefutable, as anyone who has dared to question the dominant narrative on issues from "climate change" to COVID policy to race, abortion, and identity politics will know. As I have put it in other essays, the question revolves around the location of sovereignty. Who rules? The people, articulating their interests through the metabolism of ordinary politics? Or the bureaucratic elite, who claim to discern the inevitable direction and goal of history and are prepared to marshal the coercive power of the state to prevent anyone or anything from cluttering up that highway to enlightenment? This is another description of the crossroads we face.

Can & may

In the preface to *Thoughts and Adventures*, a collection of essays published in 1932, Winston Churchill asks whether the world is "heading for the cross-roads which may lead to the two alternative Infernos," the Cities of Destruction, brought about by the engines of war, and the Cities of Enslavement, brought about by the engines of totalitarian ideology. To both, he notes, "Science holds the keys."

Some of the essays in that collection are light *jeux d'esprit* – "Hobbies," for example, and "Painting as a Pastime." Some are historical reflections, edged with political insight. But at least two bear directly on the dark crossroads Churchill adumbrates: "Shall We All Commit Suicide?" and "Fifty Years Hence." Both are remarkably prescient. Churchill speculates about the morally fraught side of technology development, a development that had accelerated suddenly within the lifetimes of his parents. Churchill dilates especially upon two things: the implications of modern technology for the practice of war and its political implications, especially in the hands of totalitarian despots who begin by vacating the central moral assumption of Christendom, that the individual possesses intrinsic – Thomas Jefferson might have said "unalienable" – moral worth.

"The story of the human race is War," Churchill acknowledges. Indeed, our species has never been notable for its pacific qualities. But it was not until the twentieth century that "War really began to enter into its kingdom as the potential destroyer of the human race." That potential was bequeathed to humanity by science. Writing in the 1920s, Churchill forecasts practically the entire twentieth-century menu of martial innovation. He imagines extraordinary developments in communications – wireless telephones, for example, which he suggests might render face-to-face meetings all but superfluous – as well as fearsome developments in chemical and biological warfare. He also notes new feats of mobilization, logistics, and brute kinetic power. How extraordinary that "it is today already possible to control accurately from the bridge of a battle cruiser all the power of hundreds of thousands of men, or to set off with one finger a mine capable in an instant of destroying the work of thousands of man years." Churchill even foresees the awesome power of nuclear energy. Might it not, he asks, be someday possible that a device no larger than an orange could destroy an entire city block or "blast a township at a stroke"? The truth is, he writes, that "Mankind has never been in this position before. Without having improved appreciably in virtue or enjoying wiser guidance, it has got into its hands for the first time the tools by which it can unfailingly accomplish its own extermination."

Churchill also understood the chilling possibilities inherent in genetic manipulation, "startling developments ... just beyond our finger-tips in the breeding of human beings and the shaping of human nature." Will it not soon be possible, for example, to produce people who possess "admirable physical development" but whose "mental endowment [is] stunted in particular directions"? "Christian civilization" recoils from such vistas, Churchill says, but "there is nothing in the philosophy of Communists to prevent their creation."

In some ways, these are by now commonplace facts about modern life. But Churchill understood that at issue was not simply the technological development of new instruments of destruction and enslavement, but a changed attitude toward humanity itself. In his book *The Abolition of Man* (1943), C. S. Lewis underscores this point. Science is about "conquering nature," Lewis acknowledges. But every victory increases the domain of that which we treat as "mere Nature," i.e., something to be mastered. "It is in Man's power," Lewis writes, "to treat himself as a mere 'natural object' and his own judgments of value as raw material for scientific manipulation to alter at will."

The frightening moral developments that writers as different as C. S. Lewis, Churchill, and Christopher Dawson foresaw have borne poisonous fruit only with recent technical innovations. But the attitudes, the view of nature and humanity that is presupposed by such developments, have their roots in the intellectual revolutions of the sixteenth and seventeenth centuries, the revolutions of "the new science," of Copernicus and Galileo, of Bacon, Newton, and Descartes. In seizing the freedom to determine itself, humanity at the same time began to assert its freedom to take charge of nature.

It would be difficult to overestimate the importance of this shift. Since the time of Aristotle, science had been essentially a contemplative matter; truth was conceived as a stable order that man strove to *behold*. But in the modern age, science became fundamentally aggressive, inseparable from the project of grasping and manipulating nature – including man's nature – according to human designs. Instead of opening himself up to nature's secrets, man now strove to *reconstruct* those secrets by active intervention. Francis Bacon's celebrated declaration to the effect that "knowledge is power" typifies the new approach.

Lewis makes the arresting observation that "there is something which unites magic and applied science while separating both from the 'wisdom' of earlier ages." It is this: "For the wise men of old," Lewis notes, the cardinal problem had been how to conform the soul to reality, and the solution had been knowledge, self-discipline, and virtue. For magic and applied science alike the problem is how to subdue reality to the wishes of men: the solution is a technique; and both, in the practice of this technique, are ready to do things hitherto regarded as disgusting and impious – such as digging up and mutilating the dead.

Lewis goes on the compare Bacon with Marlowe's Dr. Faustus, whose chief aim is not knowledge (as is sometime claimed) but power. "A sound magician," Faustus boasts, "is a mighty god."

Nowhere was this new approach more dramatically crystallized – or more systematically worked out – than in the philosophy of René Descartes, who can with some justice be considered the architect of modern science. In a famous passage near the end of the *Discourse on Method* (1637), Descartes heralds a "practical philosophy" that, unlike the speculative philosophy of scholasticism,

> would show us the energy and action of fire, air, and stars, the heavens, and all other bodies in our environment, as distinctly as we know the various crafts of our artisans, and could apply them in the same way to all appropriate uses and thus make ourselves the masters and owners of nature.

To make ourselves the "masters and owners of nature": that is the goal. The index of knowledge here is not accurate theory but power and control. Like the artisan, we really know something when we know how to make it. And among the benefits that Descartes envisioned from his new philosophy was a more efficacious medicine: by understanding the principles of nature, Descartes wrote, we might hope to control man's physical nature, freeing him from "an infinitude of maladies both of body and mind, and even also possibly of the infirmities of age."

The staggering success of modern science and technology – including modern medical technology – underscores the power and truth in some respects of Descartes' vision. What we call the modern world is in a deep sense a Cartesian world, a world in which humanity has exploited the principles outlined by Descartes to remake reality in its own image.

But there is, as Churchill, C. S. Lewis, and others have pointed out, a dark side to this mastery. Increasingly, one confronts the fear that humanity, despite its technical prowess, may be enslaved by its dominion over nature. "If man chooses to treat himself as raw material," Lewis writes, then "raw material he will be." Nor is this fear confined to the *effects* of our science, to the lethal arsenal of weapons and pollutants that human ingenuity has scattered over the face of the earth. Equally (if more subtly) fearsome is the crisis in *values* that modern science has helped to precipitate. Committed to the ideal of objectivity, of treating everything as "raw material," modern science requires that the world be silent about "values," about meaning in any human sense, for it requires that everyday experience be reduced to the ghostly, "value-free" language of primary qualities and mathematical formulae. While this language has given man great power over the world, it cannot speak to him of his place in the world.

Hence, as Nietzsche saw with devastating clarity, the other side of our commitment to the ideal of objective truth is nihilism.

"All science," Nietzsche wrote in *On the Genealogy of Morality,* "has at present the object of dissuading man from his former respect for himself, as if this had been nothing but a bizarre conceit." Since the truth for Nietzsche – as for us as well – means first of all objective, scientific truth, everything that binds us to the world as wanting, lacking, embodied creatures (sexual attraction, beauty, pain, hunger, respect) must be denied the title of truth. It was precisely this insight that led Nietzsche to insist that "the value of truth must for once be *experimentally called into question.*"

Many people are worried about the ethical implications of genetic engineering. They read about cloning or "harvesting" embryos for genetic material and wonder whether we have not started firmly down the path described by Aldous Huxley in his 1932 novel *Brave New World* or foreseen by Churchill in "Fifty Years Hence." Today we cull certain biological material from so-called "dispensable" embryos; tomorrow might we not have factories for the production of children carefully segregated according to genetic endowment?

But if many people worry about what genetic engineering portends, others face that crossroads and worry primarily about what public anxiety over such scientific research will mean for the progress of science. Such people are not necessarily insensitive to ethical issues, but for them the search for scientific truth is ineluctable. Public opinion might delay the march of progress. It will never entirely derail it. So (they argue) it behooves us to pursue science wherever it leads. If we don't, someone else will, and we in the West are better equipped than anyone to deploy new technologies wisely and humanely. To oppose the application of genetic engineering (the argument goes) is to be a latter-day Luddite, railing impotently against a technology whose effects might be painful at first but will ultimately be liberating.

It is a mistake to reject casually either side of the argument: those who worry about genetic engineering, or those who worry about the worriers. Consider the plus side. The therapeutic promise of genetic engineering is more than enormous: it is staggering. No one who has seen somebody suffer from Parkinson's Disease or any of the many other horrific ills that the flesh is heir to can be deaf to that promise.

Of course, any powerful technology can be put to evil purposes as well as good ones. In this sense, one might say that technology is like fire. It is neither good nor bad in itself. It is good when used appropriately for good purposes, bad when used inappropriately or for evil purposes. It would be pleasing to think that we could apply some such calculus to determine the moral complexion of a particular application of genetic engineering.

It is not at all clear, however, that the moral quandaries with which genetic engineering (for example) confronts us can be solved by such a calculus. Part of the problem is that the creed – familiar to us from Marxism – that "the end justifies the means" seems particularly barbarous when applied directly to human reality, as it is in genetic engineering. Are all embryos potential candidates for "harvesting," or only certain embryos? And what about newborns, another good source of genetic material? Are certain infants to be regarded as potential "raw material" for genetic experimentation? Which infants? It is easy to conjure up a nightmare world in which some human beings are raised for spare parts (and Kazuo Ishiguro did just that in a recent novel).

Already in certain parts of the world, the bodies of executed criminals are raided for kidneys, corneas, and other body parts. Why not extend the practice? According to some news reports, the Chinese already have.

In his essay "D'Holbach's Dream: The Central Claim of the Enlightenment," the Australian philosopher David Stove asked a relevant question. Granted the enormous contribution of science and technology to human happiness in the last few hundred years, how can we be sure that period was "a *typical* specimen of the effect of scientific progress on human happiness"? Perhaps, Stove suggests, it was "a lucky accident" and we have now "returned to the state, historically the more usual one, in which any progress that knowledge makes does not much increase either human happiness or misery? Have we entered a period in which scientific progress will enormously increase misery?" No one knows the answer to these questions, but it would be silly to dismiss them out of hand.

My own belief is that humanity, as Churchill discerned, is at the crossroads of an awesome moral divide. Recent advances in the technologies of artificial intelligence and genetic engineering – cloning, stem-cell research, and the like – confront us with moral problems for which we have no ready-made solution. Perhaps the biggest problem concerns the nature of the technologies involved. When we look back over the course of technological development, especially in the last couple hundred years, it is easy to be a technological optimist. Science and technology have brought us so many extraordinary advances that one is tempted to close one's eyes and take a leap of faith when it comes to the subject. No doubt science and technology have brought us many destructive things, but who except the hermits among us would willingly do without the conveniences – including lifesaving conveniences –

they have bequeathed us? It is impossible, I think, for any rational person to say "No" to science and technology. The benefits are simply too compelling. Indeed, as Churchill noted already back in the 1920s, mankind has become so dependent upon the fruits of scientific progress that "if it stopped or were reversed," there would be a "catastrophe of unimaginable horror." We have, Churchill wrote, "gone too far to go back.... There are too many people maintained, not merely in comfort but in existence, by processes unknown a century ago, for us to afford even a temporary check."

But can we afford to acquiesce and issue an indiscriminate "Yes" to scientific progress? Churchill went on to warn that "It would be much better to call a halt in material progress and discovery rather than to be mastered by our apparatus and the forces which it directs." Was he right? "There are secrets," he continued, "too mysterious for man in his present state to know, secrets which, once penetrated, may be fatal to human happiness and glory." Already, "scientists are ... fumbling with the keys of all the chambers hitherto forbidden to mankind." Yet "without an equal growth of Mercy, Pity, Peace and Love, Science herself may destroy all that makes human life majestic and tolerable."

It would be difficult to formulate sentences more thoroughly at odds with the technological spirit of our age. But can we simply dismiss Churchill's concerns? Are there not lines to be drawn, limits to be respected? If so, where do we find the criteria for drawing those lines and limits? There is no simple or pat answer to such questions. Perhaps the one thing that is certain is that we are operating here in a realm beyond certainty. No one will come up with a formula that can be successfully applied to all cases.

There are two dangers. One is the danger of technophobia:

retreating from science and technology because of the moral enormities it makes possible. The other, perhaps more prevalent danger, is technophilia, best summed up in the belief that "if it *can* be done, it *may* be done." There are many things that we can do that we ought not do. But whence does that "ought" acquire its traction and legitimacy? As science and technology develop, we find ourselves wielding ever greater power. The dark side of power is the temptation to forget its limitations. Lord Acton was right to warn that "Power corrupts, and absolute power corrupts absolutely." That observation has relevance in the world of science and technology as well as politics. None of us, of course, really commands absolute power. Our mortality assures that for all of us – rich and poor, famous and obscure – life will end in the absolute weakness of death.

But the exercise of power can be a like a drug, dulling us to the fact of our ultimate impotence. It is when we forget our impotence that we do the most damage with the power we wield. At the end of his book *Main Currents of Marxism* (1978), the Polish philosopher Leszek Kolakowski observed that "The self-deification of mankind, to which Marxism gave philosophical expression, has ended in the same way as all such attempts, whether individual or collective: it has revealed itself as the farcical aspect of human bondage." It would be a mistake to think that Marxism has a monopoly on the project of self-deification. It is a temptation as old as mankind itself. The Greeks called it hubris. And the Book of Genesis warns us about such hubris with the story of the serpent's promise to Eve: "Ye shall be as gods."

If that seems hyperbolic, consider Yuval Noah Harari, the Davos-friendly, best-selling author of pop-philosophy books warning – or crowing (it's not always easy to tell) – that human beings are just about to exceed their shelf life and need to be replaced by something better. "We are really acquiring divine powers of creation and destruction," he said in a recent interview. "We are really upgrading humans into gods." "Upgrading."

Because humans are now "hackable animals," Harari argues, they will soon grow out of their attachment to outmoded ideas such as the worth of the individual and free will. Such ideas were OK for people like Locke, Rousseau, and Thomas Jefferson, he admits, but thanks to technological advances we've gone beyond all that. "That's over," he says about the idea of free will.

It's all quite breathtaking. "The most important question in 21st-century economics," Harari writes in the best tech-mandarin style, "may well be what to do with all the superfluous people." There will be so many "superfluous" people, you see, because only a small portion of humanity will be "upgraded" to be "super-humans" who will "enjoy unheard-of abilities and unprecedented creativity, which will allow them to go on making many of the most important decisions in the world." People, it goes without saying, like Yuval Noah Harari.

All of which is to say that modern technology has upped the ante on hubris. Our amazing technological prowess seduces many people into thinking we are or, with just a bit more tinkering, might become "as gods." The first step in that process is to believe that one is exempt from normal moral limits: that "if it *can* be done, it *may* be done" – i.e., the capacity to do something brings with it the moral sanction to do it. It is a foolish thought, a dangerous thought. But it is a thought with which we will all find ourselves having to contend as we continue to surprise ourselves with our strange cleverness. It is part of the crossroads at which the West finds itself today.

CONTRIBUTORS

MICHAEL ANTON is a Lecturer in Politics and a Research Fellow at Hillsdale College's Washington, D.C., campus.

CONRAD BLACK is a financier, author, and columnist for a number of publications in Canada, the United States, and the United Kingdom. His most recent books are *Donald J. Trump: A President like No Other* and *The Canadian Manifesto*. He has been a member of the British House of Lords since 2001.

ANGELO M. CODEVILLA (1943–2021) was a Senior Fellow of the Claremont Institute and a professor emeritus at Boston University.

ANTHONY DANIELS is a contributing editor of *City Journal*.

ALLEN C. GUELZO is the Thomas W. Smith Distinguished Research Scholar & Director of the Initiative on Politics and Statesmanship in the James Madison Program in American Ideals and Institutions at Princeton University.

JAMES HANKINS is a Professor of History at Harvard University.

VICTOR DAVIS HANSON is a Senior Fellow at the Hoover Institution, Stanford University, and the author, most recently, of *The Dying Citizen* (Basic Books).

CONTRIBUTORS

ROGER KIMBALL is the editor of *The New Criterion* and publisher of Encounter Books.

JAMES PANERO is the executive editor of *The New Criterion*.

JAMES PIERESON is a Senior Fellow at the Manhattan Institute.

ANDREW ROBERTS is the Roger and Martha Mertz Visiting Fellow at the Hoover Institution.

INDEX

INDEX

Cicero, 7, 18, 103

citizenship: American (assault on), 87–95; efforts of elites to curb or replace, 91; enemies of, 108; rebirth of, 105–8; risk to survival of, 95; Western (early, challenges to), 100–105; Western (origins of), 95–100

civilization: alternative, 186; dynamism vs. stasis, 199; formula for decline of, 187; foundational pillar of, 58; fragility of, xi, 6; prerequisites for the perpetuation of, x; terms defining, 177; undercutting of (by ruling class), 49. *See also* birth, benefits, and burden of Western civilization; Chinese civilization, specter of; culture against civilization; tradition, civilization and

Civil War, 107, 140

class warfare. *See* overclass, going under with

Cleopatra, 112

climate change: concerns about, 193; questioning of dominant narrative on, 208

Clinton, Bill, 73, 148

Codevilla, Angelo M., 48–66

Cold War: forecasts dismissed amidst the reality of, 180; threat posed by communism during, 179; victory in, 142, 148; view of the future during, 193

Columbus, Christopher, 123

communism: China's scrapping of (as economic policy), 182; China's transition to, 52; as fighting faith, 180; international (collapse of), 129, 181; Muhammad of Communism (Lenin as), 30; search for transcendence amidst (continuation of), 32; threat posed by (during Cold War), 179, 193

Confucius, 50, 51

Connolly, Cyril, 198

Constitution, 107, 177, 205

Coptic Church, 116

covid-19 epidemic: efforts to discredit non-favored ideas about, 59; "Great Reset" announced in the wake of, 205; illegal immigrants not tested for covid, 75, 90; meting out of scare treatments during, 157; questioning of dominant narrative on, 208; Western world worn ragged by, 130

Critical Race Theory, 75, 165–66, 171

cultural amnesia, ix

culture against civilization, 176–95; adversaries of culture, 182–89; alternative civilization, 186; American prosperity (golden age of), 192; bipartisan compromise (lack of efforts toward), 189; Capitol riots (January 6, 2021), 190; civilization (terms defining), 177; climate change (concerns about), 193; coalition-building (Democrats'), 188; Cold War, 179, 193; communism (fear of), 180; Constitution (faith in), 177; Democratic Party (remaking of), 188; distinguished tradition (collapse of), 176; diversity (devolution of culture into doctrine known as), 186; diversity ideology (expression of decadence in), 195; diversity ideology (as operating doctrine of the Democratic Party), 188, 193; dystopian novel (Orwell), 179; eruption of protests, 182–83; grim picture, 190–92; identity politics (attempts to hold debates about), 187; inflation, 191; international communism (collapse of), 181; Kavanaugh hearings, 190; labor productivity, 181;

INDEX

Franklin, Benjamin, 137, 138
French and Indian War, 138
French Revolution, 54
Frost, Robert, 197
Fukuyama, Francis, 129, 148

Galileo, 123
Gandhi, 193
Gender Queer: A Memoir, 77
genetic engineering, 214–16
George III (king), 139
Gibbon, 105
Gilbert, W. S., 33
God: death of, 31; same (humans as creatures of), 58
Google, censorship by, 63, 64
Gordon, Robert, 192
Great Depression, 107, 148
Great Enrichment, 23, 24
"Great Replacement," 74
Great Reset (as new crossroads), 94, 205
"green-energy" agenda, 206
Guelzo, Allen C., ix, x, xi, 1–25, 200

Hadrian, 145
Hankins, James, ix, x, xi, 1–25, 200
Hannah-Jones, Nikole, 155
Hanson, Victor Davis, 87–108
Harari, Yuval Noah, 218, 219
Harper's, 158
Hecate, 197, 198
Hellenic civilization, 8
Hemings, Sally, 140
Herodotus, 10, 100
Hobbes, Thomas, 118
Horace, 8
hubris, 4, 197, 218–19
Hume, David, 44

humility: malicious form of, xi; proper, 5, 6; warranted, 108
Huxley, Aldous, 47, 214

identity politics, 87, 200, 208; attempts to hold debates about, 187; benefit to elites from culture of, 173; "intolerance and racism" at the heart of, 170; tribalism vs., 91
ideology. *See* monomania, popular form of
indispensable country, 128–51; Abolitionist Society of Pennsylvania, 140; accomplishments, 141; Afghan errors, 133–36; al Qaeda, 133; American decline (appearance of), 136, 149; Biden administration, 151; Black Lives Matter, 131; China (arrival of), 128; China (generosity of Western powers abused by), 130; Civil War, 140; Cold War, 142; country not imploding (United States as), 136–43; covid crisis, 130; crossroads, 143–47; disconcerting phenomena, 131; establishment slur, 150; European Union (secession of the United Kingdom from), 145; geopolitical health of America, 144; inflation, 131; international communism (collapse of), 129; Iran nuclear agreement, 149; Jefferson's egalitarianism, 139; Keystone XL oil pipeline (Biden's stopping of), 132; Middle East (war in), 148; NATO, 133–35; Obamacare, 149; "peaceful protests" (summer of 2020), 131; political generals (Rome), 147; recent regression, 147–51; rights asserted by the West, 128; Roman Empire, decline of (comparisons to), 145;

INDEX

Index

utopia (*cont.*)
  "unprecedented" situation, 202;
  "upgrading" of humans, 219; war, 209;
  woke educationists (Princeton), 199
vainglory, 4
"Varsity Blues" scandal, 167
very simple principle (Mills), 41, 44
Vikings, 119–20
virtue(s): civic, 153; measure of, 32, 38;
  opinion as metonym for, 33; Sermon-
  on-the-Mount, 104; strength of
  offense as sign of commitment to, 44
Voltaire, 204

Wall Street Journal, 201
*War That Made the Roman Empire:
  Antony, Cleopatra, and Octavian at
  Actium, The* (Strauss), 114
Washington, George, 135, 138, 141
The West that Wasn't, 109–27; Actium,
  114, 124; Albinonic Fringe (Viking
  presence at), 119, 125; Alexander the
  Great, 112; Arianism, 116; "Before the
  Coptic Era," 111; Christopher Colum-
  bis, 123; Cleopatra, 112–13; Coptic
  Church, 116; counterfactual history,
  110; Dar-al-Islam, 119, 121, 124, 126;
  Dark Ages, 118; democracy (Athenian
  empire rid of), 111; Druids, 118;
  Empire of Mali, 121; Five Empires,
  122; Galileo, 123; "global East" (dominance of), 125; great earthquake, 118;
  "hinge" of history, 114; "Holy Fire,"
  121; Islam (advent of), 119; "liberal
  values," 124; library at Alexandria,
115–16; Marcus Pontius Pilate, 117;
Mark Anthony, 112–13; Peloponnesian
Wars, 111; popular obscurantism, 123;
Ptolemaic Empire, 112, 115; puerperal
fever (elimination of), 120; Renæssance, 122, 125; representational government, 125; Roman Empire (ascent
of), 112; Roman Empire (death throes
of), 117; Ronald Reagan, 124;
"sauna," 120; scholarship (aim of),
110; "Skraelings," 120; spiritual toleration, 116; Stonehenge, 118; technology,
124–25; "Viking Surge," 120; wealth
(meaningful), 124; Western achievements, 126–27; Yin China, 125
Wilberforce, William, 46
Williams, Thomas Chatterton, 175
Wilson, Woodrow, 142
woke educationists (Princeton), 199
wokeness, 87, 90, 200
Woke Racism (McWhorter), 171
woke regime (eventual collapse of), 65
woke tyranny, 49
Wolfe, Tom, 154
World War I, 107, 128, 141, 198
World War II, 107, 128–29, 141
Wright brothers, 121

Xenophon, 20, 100

Yale Daily News, 166
Year Zero, 84

Zhou Enlai, 52
Zinn, Howard, 139

234

A NOTE ON THE TYPE

W HERE N EXT? *has been set in Darden Studio's Corundum Text,*
a family of types derived from the work of Pierre-Simon Fournier le
jeune. Fournier's achievement as a typographer is best known in the
form of Monotype's interpretation of the "Saint Augustin Ordi-
naire" types shown in his 1725 Manuel Typographique. *Cut under*
Stanley Morison's direction in 1925–26, the Monotype version –
christened "Fournier" – was under development at the same time
as a somewhat darker type that would eventually be given the name
Barbou in honor of the publisher of Fournier's Traité historique sur
l'origine et les progrès des caractères de font pour l'impression de
la musique *(1765), which provided Morison's models for the types.*
Morison would have preferred to release Barbou to the printing
trade, but a misunderstanding during his absence from the works
led to the release of Fournier. But for a handful of appearances,
Barbou largely disappeared from view. The present version of the
type captures the rich color of the eighteenth-century original and
maintains its lively spirit, especially in the italics.

DESIGN & COMPOSITION BY CARL W. SCARBROUGH